THE MOST AUTHORITATIVE AND ACCESSIBLE GUIDE
FOR MANAGING YOUR CHURCH

essential guide to
Church Finances

RICHARD J. VARGO, MBA, PH.D. & VONNA LAUE, MBA, CPA

www.YourChurchResources.com

essential guide to
Church Finances

Copyright © 2009 Your Church Resources/Christianity Today International. All rights reserved.

We grant permission for material in this book to be photocopied for use in a local church setting, provided that:
1. no more than 1,000 copies are made;
2. the material is distributed free and no charge is made for admission to the class or event; and
3. the copies include the notice, "Copyright © 2009 Your Church Resources/Christianity Today International. Reprinted from *Essential Guide to Church Finances*."

No part of this book may be reproduced, stored in a retrieval system, or transmitted, in any form or by any means, electronic, mechanical, photocopying, recording, or otherwise, without prior written permission from the publisher, except as noted above and in the case of brief quotations embodied in critical articles and reviews.

For any other use, including tuition-based classroom use, advance permission must be obtained from the copyright holder. For information, contact:

Your Church Resources Permissions
Christianity Today International
465 Gundersen Drive
Carol Stream, IL 60188
Phone: (877) 247-4787
E-mail: clttodaycustserv@christianitytoday.com

This publication is designed to provide accurate and authoritative information in regard to the subject matter covered. It is sold with the understanding that the publisher is not engaged in rendering legal, accounting, or other specific service. If legal advice or other expert assistance is required, the services of a competent professional person should be sought. From a *Declaration of Principles jointly adopted by a Committee of the American Bar Association and a Committee of Publishers and Associates.*

Visit our website, YourChurchResources.com

Credits
    Authors: Richard J. Vargo, MBA, Ph.D.
                Vonna Laue, MBA, CPA
     Editor: Marian V. Liautaud
Art Director: Phil Marcelo
Cover image: Brand X Pictures; Dave Allen Photography/ iStockphoto

0-917463-51-x
978-0-917463-51-8

11 10 09   1 2 3 4
Printed in the United States of America.

About the authors:

Richard J. Vargo, M.B.A., Ph.D., is a professor of accounting in the Eberhardt School of Business at the University of the Pacific, Stockton, California. He is the recipient of the prestigious Accounting Faculty Merit Award given by the California Society of Certified Public Accountants for his contributions to accounting education in California.

> *To my wife, Melinda, thank you for your love, support, and editorial assistance on this book and its predecessors.* —Richard J. Vargo

Vonna Laue is licensed as a California and Colorado CPA and is a member of the American Institute of Certified Public Accountants, the Society for Human Resource Management and the National Association of Church Business Administration. She is a partner with the nonprofit accounting firm, Capin Crouse, which she joined in 1996, and she serves clients including churches, colleges, universities, seminaries, mission organizations, and other nonprofit ministries. Vonna obtained a Masters in Business Administration in Leadership and Human Resource Management from the University of Colorado.

> *I wouldn't be equipped for this type of endeavor if it wasn't for the firm of Capin Crouse and their mission of serving ministries with excellence. To my husband, Bryan, thank you for supporting me no matter how hard I try to run and for gently pulling me back when my balance meter isn't functioning properly. I am blessed beyond words to be your wife. Bethany and Kimberly, you're the joy in our lives and I can't wait to see how God continues to use you to impact others.* —Vonna Laue

We would like to thank the following individuals for their time and helpful feedback on early drafts of this book:

Michael E. Batts, CPA, Managing Shareholder, Batts, Morrison, Wales & Lee, P.A.
Anne Kessler, Business Manager, Church of the Resurrection
Brian McAuliffe, CFO & Director of Operations, Willow Creek Community Church
Pete McCarty, Executive Director of Finance, The Chapel
Elaine Sommerville, CPA, Sommerville & Associates, P.C.

Preface

Churches are one of the most complex financial organizations on the planet. What other entity lives or dies primarily by weekly donor giving, recruits untrained volunteers to manage large sums of money, and requires specialized experience in nonprofit tax law and federal reporting requirements, in which few individuals, let alone professionals, have expertise.

Years ago, Richard Vargo created a three-book primer on church finances. His series, which included *Church Financial Reporting*, *Church Planning & Budgeting*, and *Internal Controls*, has provided timeless truths for church financial leaders. Written with the novice volunteer bookkeeper or treasurer in mind, Richard's work has proven to be evergreen; it continues to provide the best starting point for churches that want to establish sound financial practices.

This new volume—*Essential Guide to Church Finances*—blends a newly edited version of Richard's original resources, updated for today's churches, along with two new chapters from Vonna Laue, a CPA with the nonprofit accounting firm, Capin Crouse. Together, these two authors bring a balance of technical understanding of accounting principles and the application of these concepts based on firsthand experience working with churches that are striving to get their financial houses in order.

This book primarily is written for church staff and volunteers who need an overview of the essential information for managing church finances along with practical examples for how to put these principles into play. Church financial leaders often will come to their position in the church with professional experience in the for-profit sector. Not all of the principles and practices that applied in this realm will transfer to church work. This book will serve as a good transitional guide to help acclimate staff and volunteers to the nuances of nonprofit work.

From basics to best practices, each chapter includes action items to discuss as a team and implement. The book is loaded with sample forms, reports, and checklists, all designed to equip you with the tools you need to protect the financial well-being of your ministry.

We hope this book blesses you and the church where you serve. As with all of our resources, we'd love to know how this book has helped you, or what we can do to improve its usefulness before our next print run. Until then, God bless you as you strive to serve your church, which Christ has raised up for His glory!

Marian V. Liautaud

Editor, *Essential Guide to Church Finances*

Table of Contents

Table of Contents

Preface   **vii**

1. Church Planning and Budgeting   1

1. **Resource Allocation** 2
   - Accountability............................ 2
   - Terminology 2

2. **Meeting at St. Chaos Church** 4
   - Summary: A Checklist of Ten Common Budgeting Mistakes 7

3. **Planning: The Birthplace Of Specific, Measurable Goals And Objectives** 7
   - Keys To Proper Planning.................... 8
   - Evaluation of Progress 8
   - Long-range Planning 9

4. **Budgeting**............................10
   - Power of a Name.......................... 13

5. **Budget Directions** 14
   - Top-Down Approach...................... 14
   - Bottom-Up Approach 15
   - First Church 16

6. **Budget Approaches**......................16
   - Incremental Budgeting 17
   - Program Budgeting 17

7. **The Annual Operating Budget**................21
   - Budget Estimation 21
   - The Annual Budgeting Process and Timetable .. 22
   - Budgeting for the Inflow of Resources 24
   - Weekly Offerings 24
   - Restricted Gifts 27
   - Pastor's Discretionary Fund 27
   - Donated Services 28
   - Budgeting for the Outflow of Resources........ 28
   - Games People Play........................ 30

8. **Other Budgets**...........................30
   - Monthly Cash Budget 30
   - Capital-Spending Budget.................... 31
   - Debt Retirement Budget 32
   - Some Observations........................ 32

9. **Structure For Change** 32

2. Performance Measurements   37

1. **How are you doing?** 38

2. **Inward Comparisons—A place to start** 39

3. **Comparative Ratios—How do we measure up against other churches?** 41

4. **Peer Group Comparison**.....................43
   - Ratios Based On The Statement Of Financial Position 43
   - Ratios Based On The Statement Of Activities................................ 45
   - Additional Ratios 48

3. Church Financial Reporting   63

1. **Effective Financial Reporting**................64

2. **Communication: The Reason To Report**........64

3. **Principles Of Financial Reporting**.............67
   - Responsibility Reporting.................... 68
   - Exception Reporting 68
   - Summarized Reporting..................... 68
   - Comparative Reporting..................... 68
   - Interpretive Reporting...................... 69
   - Other Factors in Financial Reporting 69

4. Different Audiences, Different Reports 71
- Reporting to the General Membership 71
- Reporting to Management 74
- Reporting to Others 76

5. Structure For Change 77

4. Internal Financial Controls to Minimize the Risk of Embezzlement 85

1. Internal Control Of Assets 86

2. General Objectives Of Internal Financial Control .. 86

3. Internal Control Problems In Churches 87
- Causes and Some Suggestions 87
- Separation of Duties....................... 88
- Establishment of a Clear Organizational Structure..................... 89
- Recruitment of Qualified Personnel 89
- Accounting Procedures Manual.............. 90
- Absence of Monitoring 91
- The Arena of Trust 91

4. Internal Control Systems 92

5. 50 Internal Control Practices For Every Church: A Test 93
- Internal Controls: General 93
- Internal Controls: Cash Receipts 97
- Internal Controls: Cash Disbursements 102
- Internal Controls: Reconciliation Practices 108
- Internal Controls: Other Assets 112
- Test Results 114

5. Audits 117

1. General Overview 118

2. Compliance Audits 118
- Avoiding An Audit........................ 119
- Surviving An Audit 121

3. Internal Audits 121
- St. Chaos Undergoes An Internal Audit 122

4. External Audits........................128
- Beginning The Process..................... 129
- Selecting An Auditor 129
- Preparation For The Audit 129
- Management Comment Letter 130
- After The Audit........................... 132
- Board Presentation........................ 132

6. Index 141

Chapter 1

Church Planning and Budgeting

by Richard J. Vargo

1. RESOURCE ALLOCATION

All organizations have a limited amount of resources with which to operate. Thus Microsoft, school districts, retail stores, service clubs, families and churches all have at least one financial element in common: the need to achieve their goals and objectives with limited resources. Just as you must exhibit some restraint in your personal spending in order to have enough money for clothing, shelter, transportation, and recreation for your family, churches too must be cautious in allocating their resources among programs. Unfortunately, as long as the Church has existed, there have always been more hurts and hopes to address than resources available. Because church resources are limited and, in most cases, represent funds entrusted to the church by the congregation, church officials have a special fiduciary responsibility to make sure that every nickel of these funds is spent wisely.

ACCOUNTABILITY

Spending money wisely is not the same as simply spending money. Most churches have a budgeting, accounting, and financial reporting system to show how they plan to spend money and then to prove how the money is actually spent. Unfortunately, many churches mistakenly think that accounting is the same as accountability. Church financial administrators will often spend hours pouring over the reports to make certain that all expenditures have been recorded properly and are shown correctly in the reports. Heaven help the church accountant who misclassifies an expenditure! Having expenditures show up in the church's financial reports in the proper account and in the correct amount is good accounting, to be sure. But real accountability involves measuring whether the church has met its goals and objectives by wisely spending its resources.

Churches can usually show that they have specific programs and that money has been spent and correctly accounted for, but they typically cannot show whether the funds have been wisely spent. Spending money wisely involves *both* establishing specific, measurable goals and objectives and then, after spending the money, evaluating whether the church's goals and objectives have been met by spending the money.

To illustrate this point, let's presume that the church started a hot lunch program for elderly people in the community and budgeted $12,000 for this purpose. Further, assume that during the year, only $9,700 was spent. When the financial report of the program is received by the church officials, many are likely to praise the program coordinator's ability to operate the program under budget. But would the officials be as kind if, for example, they also found out that only eight people a day were served and that the meal was always the finest steak? Alternatively, would they be pleased if several hundred seniors were fed daily but only bologna sandwiches were served? The answer is probably "no" in both cases. For although only $9,700 was spent for food, and the elderly did receive some benefit, church officials could easily argue that the church's funds were not spent wisely. A nutritionist would have a field day testing whether either of the menus described complied with the daily dietary requirements of older people. Thus we can see that a preoccupation with the amount of money spent can be misleading. Obviously, the church's hot lunch program needs a definition of purpose complemented by goals and objectives.

To repeat, spending money is not the same as spending money wisely. The accountant's role is to make certain that money is wisely spent.

TERMINOLOGY

Few churches have an on-staff accountant. Most churches have a treasurer, or a treasurer and bookkeeper (sometimes referred to as a financial secretary) to assist in the processing of routine transactions. Different churches may use different titles for persons having virtually identical financial responsibilities. Further, the manner in which accounting and financial information is reported to church officials is different among churches. Before we dive into the details on how to manage church finances, let's define roles—

who handles what aspects of your church's finances—and establish a workable organizational structure. By establishing these details up front, when reference is made to the bookkeeper, for example, all readers will visualize the same position. Example 1.1 presents the organizational structure used in this book.

Here are typical responsibilities and duties for each of these positions:

- ***Bookkeeper, or Financial Secretary*** – Maintains the accounting records (books) by recording all income and expenditure transactions, prepares disbursement checks ready for authorized signatures, and prepares financial reports. Found in large churches. Often a full-time, paid position. Reports to the treasurer.
- ***Treasurer*** – Responsible for safeguarding church assets, analyzing church programs that have financial ramifications, paying bills, and issuing financial reports. In large churches, oversees the work of the bookkeeper or financial secretary. Serves also as the bookkeeper if none exists. Reports to the finance committee.
- ***Church Business Administrator*** – Oversees day-to-day operations of the church office including non-ordained employees, finances, church property, and building and grounds. Church business administrators may or may not be ordained ministers. Reports to the senior minister or to an administrative board.
- ***Finance Committee*** – Oversees all financial activities. Receives financial reports and analysis from the treasurer and subcommittees that deal with specific financial matters such as budgeting. Makes recommendations on financial issues to the administrative board.
- ***Administrative Board*** – Oversees all church affairs. Receives reports from the finance committee as well as all other committees, such as the worship committee, the Christian education committee, the youth committee, the buildings and grounds committee, and others. Clergy often hold membership, perhaps ex officio, on this board. Reports to the congregation.

The minister or pastor is not shown on this organizational chart because different churches position that person at different levels of authority. You may add your minister or pastor to the chart at the place appropriate to your own church.

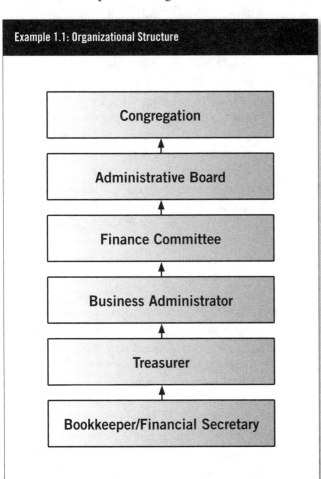

Example 1.1: Organizational Structure

- Congregation
- Administrative Board
- Finance Committee
- Business Administrator
- Treasurer
- Bookkeeper/Financial Secretary

■ ACTION ITEMS ■

- ☐ Using the descriptions provided, create your own organizational chart.
- ☐ Based on the position descriptions above, are there any gaps in responsibility on your staff that need to be assigned? Identify these areas and who will fill them.
- ☐ Are the right people in the right positions? If not, who will need to shift to provide a better match for job responsibilities?
- ☐ Is there anyone serving in a position in which they require more training or supervision? If so, determine what training is needed and how you will provide it.

2. MEETING AT ST. CHAOS CHURCH

In the following pages you will be eavesdropping on the annual budget meeting of St. Chaos Church.* Although this hypothetical church probably does not allocate its resources in exactly the same way that your church does, some similarities may exist. In fact some church members have accused me of secretly attending their meetings! As the meeting progresses, I will provide a running critique of the activities.

The chairperson of the finance committee begins. "Thanks for coming out on such a rainy day. As LSU and Ohio State are playing for the national collegiate football championship later today, let's try to wrap up our discussion of next year's budget as quickly as possible."

Critique—Budget process
As I will discuss later, the budget process should be done carefully and extend over several months. For instance, planning for the yearly operating budget should start at least six months in advance. Preparing a budget quickly is bad administration. Yet countless churches get in to the habit of doing their budgeting before sporting events, before picnics, between services, in one evening, or in other constricted timeframes. Good planning and budgeting should take awhile. These are activities where you get out of them only what you put in.

The program leader of the buildings and grounds committee requests a five percent increase over this year's operating budget plus $40,000 for a new roof and $30,000 to repave the parking lot. No report on the current year's activities is provided, the amounts for the roof and paving are rough estimates, and no details of the budget year activities are provided. "The buildings and grounds look magnificent. Let's help keep them that way," voice members of the finance committee.

---

* The idea for this budget meeting comes from a similar meeting presented in "The Evaluation of Resource Usage in the Not-for-Profit Environment," written by Loudell O. Ellis, published in *The Woman CPA*, v. 37, April 1975, 6-8.

"Your operating budget is approved. But we don't have enough funds for both the roof and repaving, so we'll give you $30,000. Either get the parking lot repaved or get a cheaper roof."

Critique—Clarify results
There are several problems with this allocation of funds.

1. *All programs being funded on a continuous yearly basis need to provide information on what was accomplished with the previously budgeted monies. Also, any request for an increase in funding must be justified. The finance committee must know in advance what results to expect from spending the additional money. It might be that volunteers could be recruited to help with buildings and grounds in order to cut costs. Certain projects might be turned over to special groups, such as teens or retired members, for low-cost completion. Perhaps even more projects could then be completed by the buildings and grounds committee for the same amount of money. Such possibilities need to be fully explored, but they don't get discussed if the goals for the next year are not "put on the table." Note that the program's leader presented no information needed to evaluate past or anticipated activities. In some churches no data means no money.*
2. *The need for a new roof and for repaving the parking lot was never established, and the amounts involved were just rough estimates. For such big budget items, the program leader should prove the need and obtain detailed estimates by licensed contractors.*
3. *For major work, the finance committee should not give such latitude concerning the use of the funds. Although there are only two choices involved, there's a hint of "Here's the money. Do what you want with it."*
4. *If $40,000 is really needed for a new roof, the $30,000 allocated is insufficient to do an adequate job. The church might be better off by waiting another year to obtain adequate funds to put on a quality roof. Provide enough money to do the job right.*

The program leader of the music committee requests a 10 percent increase over the current year's amount. The request includes $1,000 for music books, $750 for organ repairs, $500 for podiums, $2,000 for new instruments, and $30,000 for miscellaneous items related to committee activities. "Approved" says the committee.

> ### Critique—Justify expenditures
> First, to repeat an earlier discussion, the committee needs data on existing activities to determine if this year is going satisfactorily before considering the request for next year. Also, the next period's anticipated expenditures must be justified. Why new music books? What's wrong with the ones we have? What's wrong with the organ? Why new podiums and instruments?
>
> Second, miscellaneous should be the smallest of all items requested, not the largest. We need specifics on how money will be spent. Each program leader requesting funds must make a case or prove that they need exactly what they are asking for.

The bookkeeper then submits a report on the acquisition of a computer and software to handle the church's accounting needs. She had been asked to prepare the report by the finance committee. She concludes that the church needs to spend about $2,000 for a computer and $4,000 for a comprehensive software program. Her analysis of the currently available computers and computer programs is very thorough. "Thank you for the report," says a member of the finance committee, "but that's a lot of money. Let's instead appeal to the congregation to donate a computer. Then we can ask around for some software. Somebody must have something that will work."

> ### Critique—Donated equipment
> There are several mistakes in planning and budgeting here. First, if someone has taken the time to prepare a report for the meeting, the report should be reviewed as a courtesy to the preparer. If the reports are read and considered, other program leaders will notice this and the committee will receive more reports. If they are quickly discarded, few people will go to the trouble of preparing them. All budget requests must be thoroughly reviewed.
>
> Second, getting a donated computer and software might be exactly what is **not** needed. Looking to the congregation for a computer might take the decision out of the hands of the finance committee. Donations are great, as long as the items received are exactly what are needed. Using unsuitable computers, software, photocopiers, minivans, buses or other materials because they are donated might actually turn out to be a huge waste of resources. In many ways you get what you pay for. Provide enough money to purchase quality and reliable assets.

At this point in the meeting a member of the finance committee has second thoughts about the allocation of funds to the building and grounds and music committees. "Don't get me wrong. I'm all in favor of maintaining our facilities and enhancing our great music program. But shouldn't we first consider the amount of funds we will have available next year before we start to divide it up among the various programs? I think we have put the carriage in front of the horse."

"Possibly so," says another member, "but this congregation has always supported the programs approved by this committee. Don't worry; the Lord will provide."

"I guess I was out of order," says the questioning member. "Forget my comments."

> ### Critique—Forecast resources
> Actually the questioning member is making a valid point. Each church has a limited amount of resources with which to work. To maximize the possibility of success, those resources should be directed toward predetermined goals and objectives. You need to forecast the amount of resources available before committing to various programs, some of which might turn out to have long-term, high-cost needs.

The next budget request comes from the program leader of the Christian education committee. The request is well documented with data, and justifications are provided for all increases from the current year's level of expenditures. But the Christian education committee continues to request funding for a preschool program that has been funded for several years but has never been started. The committee believes that continued funding will encourage someone finally to do something about it. "Sounds reasonable," says the finance committee. "Approved."

Critique—Funding nonexistent programs
Funding a nonexistent program is dangerous. For one thing, there are no assurances that the program is needed. After all, it has been funded before and nothing happened. There's a message in that. Further, why should a program be funded before its mission and goals have been approved? Also, the existence of this budgeted amount might cause the Christian education committee to think of this money as a reserve fund in case its other educational projects are over-budget. The Christian education committee could, therefore, get sloppy in its spending habits. Additionally, funding of a nonexistent program will not be overlooked by the other program leaders. If these other leaders are short of funds later in the year, a few will inevitably request that the unused funds earmarked for the nonexistent preschool program be reallocated to their areas. Endless debates could occur at each future meeting of the finance committee.

The next request comes from a longtime senior member who wants to do something for the community's homeless persons. She's vague about what exactly she wants to do, how to do it and how much it will cost. More than anything else, she wants the church to take a position on the matter by earmarking $950 for the program. "You've got it," affirms the finance committee.

Critique—Earmarking funds blindly
Although the advocate is sincere, she simply does not yet have a fundable program. One approach is to tell her that she needs to talk with other church members and to develop a clearly defined program of assistance, together with monetary needs and program goals, to present at a future meeting of the finance committee. An alternative might be to allocate a nominal amount of seed money for her to investigate the need for and costs of such a program. You do not want to discourage new ideas for programs, but you cannot use the church's very limited resources without expecting specific results.

The worship committee is requesting an increase in its budget for next year. Its leader is convinced that a new computerized email system that touts the upcoming sermon and other Sunday activities of the church will secure a 90 percent attendance of all members at weekly worship services, up from 45 percent this year. "Approved. Great idea!"

Critique—Unrealistic expectations
One problem here is unrealistic expectations. Churches having normal attendance of less than 50 percent of members would need the proverbial miracle to double attendance in a year, regardless of what steps were taken. Rather than fund a program whose standard cannot be attained and doom the worship committee to failure, it would be more realistic to discuss a lower level of expectations, say 60 percent attendance. Expectations must be reasonable.

At this point in the meeting, a request is heard to make a donation to the election fund of a member who is running for the office of mayor. "Is it legal?" "Is it proper use of church funds?" "Can she win?" These questions are raised around the table. "She's one of us. We should support her." "Well, okay. It's only $1,000. Approved."

Critique—Spending directives
The problem here is that no one is quite sure if making the donation is an appropriate use of church funds. Essentially the members of the committee are searching for directives to guide their action. If none are available they are on their own. Several odd proposals are likely to be brought before the finance committee each year. Without specific goals and objectives to refer to, some of these requests could be funded inappropriately. Criteria must be established for the appropriate use of church funds.

Youth programs are handled by a young man who is not terribly organized. Parental support and youth involvement have decreased in recent years because of his lack of leadership. He asks for a five percent increase over this year's budget for new activities, which "will create great interest in the youth programs." Everyone on the finance committee knows that it won't help, but the request is approved.

Critique—Supporting poor leadership
The finance committee just knowingly committed itself to wasting some of the church's valuable, limited resources. A change in program leadership is needed, an unpleasant thought in most churches. But those churches addressing this issue will have more resources for other purposes.

Time is running short, but a member of the finance committee interjects that interest rates on bank certificates of deposit (CDs) have recently increased. "Why not put some of our funds in CDs and earn some interest for the future? How are we ever going to build a parsonage if we don't save any money? How about the purchase of the land adjoining the church for a larger parking area? How about providing for future generations of members? I'm afraid that by approving all of the requests, however worthy, we are draining the church of its resources. As a conservative person, I think we should invest $50,000 in CDs to ensure the future of the church."

"You have a point there. I think we should scale back all of the requests that we have just approved by ten percent and more critically evaluate the other proposals yet to be discussed," notes the chairperson. "All agreed? Yes? Great. Did all of the program leaders hear that? Who left? I'll tell them on Sunday. Moving on, the next committee is missions. . ."

SUMMARY: A CHECKLIST OF TEN COMMON BUDGETING MISTAKES

- ☐ Not allowing for enough time to prepare the budget.
- ☐ Not knowing in advance the expected results of spending money.
- ☐ Not proving the need to spend more money.
- ☐ Not providing enough money to do the job right.
- ☐ Not being specific enough about how money will be spent.
- ☐ Not properly reviewing budget requests.
- ☐ Not purchasing quality and reliable equipment.
- ☐ Not properly forecasting funds available to spend.
- ☐ Not having realistic expectations.
- ☐ Not establishing criteria for the appropriate use of church funds.

■ ACTION ITEMS ■

- ☐ What is the budget process at your church?
- ☐ As you review the checklist above, which mistakes has your church made? What was the outcome of these mistakes?
- ☐ Based on these ten mistakes, write down an action plan for every budget planning item that needs to be addressed. For instance, if you do not currently allow enough time to prepare the annual budget, determine a more appropriate timeline.

3. PLANNING: THE BIRTHPLACE OF SPECIFIC, MEASURABLE GOALS AND OBJECTIVES

Many of the problems of St. Chaos related to poor planning and a lack of clear-cut goals and objectives. The finance committee of St. Chaos was simply not ready to allocate the church's resources among programs. They didn't know where they were headed or how they were going to get there. Unfortunately, many churches skip the planning phase of the accounting and financial reporting process. An analogy might be helpful.

Clear and shared focus
Assume that you visit the corporate headquarters of XYZ Company, a toy manufacturer, to question employees on the company's goals and objectives. During the course of your visit, you hear many comments on

the need to increase sales, cut costs, increase productivity, advertise more effectively, increase market share, and so on. On closer inspection you find that all of these comments relate to the objective of increasing the profits of the firm. Rightly or wrongly, employees are rewarded, promoted, laid off, retired early, or fired based on how they contribute (or fail to contribute) to the so-called "bottom line" profit. That's the way it is in the profit sector. Few persons working for profit-seeking businesses fail to grasp the company's key business objective. The capitalist system efficiently focuses the attention of all personnel on a common, measurable objective.

General versus specific goals

In nonprofit organizations, churches included, no such common focus exists. Thus each organization must force itself to spend time in planning and, as an outgrowth, in developing its own goals and objectives to guide its every action. It is only then that programs can be developed to achieve these goals and objectives.

Without adequate planning, you can easily slide into a situation like the one illustrated by St. Chaos. For example, in a recent church administration seminar, I asked all attendees (treasurers, bookkeepers, pastors, assistant pastors, administrative board members, and others) to list the five main goals and objectives of their churches in decreasing order of priority. Several people chuckled. Several people thought it an appropriate time to go to the restroom or to get something to drink. Those few who were mentally committed to the task had great difficulty getting beyond the first few goals. After several minutes we shared the results of the exercise by discussing the lists.

Typically, the initial goal and objective related to the continued belief in and support of Christian principles, including the Bible as the word of God. Beyond that the responses became more scattered and were often expressed as generalized activities, such as evangelism, youth activities, helping people, or membership growth. Further, even when five goals and objectives were given, few attendees could establish priorities within their lists. Comments such as, "They are all important," were common. Yet, faced with limited resources, church officials need to handle high-priority objectives before spending money on low-priority objectives. Not a single objective on anyone's list was measurable. It was as if merely having activities that addressed religious and social concerns was enough. Trying is not the same as achieving.

Without proper planning, goals are dreams, objectives are hazy, programs are vague, priorities are confused, and evaluations are impossible. In such an environment, accounting is relegated to the role of making sure that any funds that are spent are accounted for properly, not that the funds are spent wisely.

The successful church establishes specific, well-thought-out objectives in the same way that a sharpshooter aims a rifle at a target. And like the sharpshooter hitting the target, the successful church knows when its objective has been achieved and when it hasn't. Alternatively, an unsuccessful church offers generalized objectives (i.e. to assist, to help out, to benefit, to do good work, etc.) without any thought of ever evaluating the progress toward meeting the objectives. Using the target analogy, it's like shooting in the general direction of the target with a shotgun.

KEYS TO PROPER PLANNING

Operating as they do in the nonprofit sector, and usually with a large cadre of volunteers who need focus, it is imperative that churches aim for their target based on planning. Proper planning involves:

- ☐ Identifying needs
- ☐ Stating goals – statement of intent and direction
- ☐ Stating objectives – the desired ends that are to be achieved in a specific period of time
- ☐ Being specific (as opposed to generalizing)
- ☐ Establishing priorities
- ☐ Being able to evaluate progress toward reaching the goals and objectives
- ☐ Considering both short-term and long-term perspectives

EVALUATION OF PROGRESS

Because churches do not provide tangible products or services, evaluating the progress of churches in achieving their ministry is not an easy task. After all, how do you determine that worship services are truly effective, that the choral music couldn't be better, that the value of pastoral counseling to a teenager in difficulty was a success, or that a program to assist flood victims was successful? Even though it's very difficult, we cannot sidestep the problem of measurement by claiming, as many do, that "our church is growing while it is doing worthwhile, noble, and helpful things for its members and the community at large." Perhaps the growth is due to being located in a high-growth town and the church would prosper even if its programs were of dubious quality.

Ministry metrics

Evaluation of progress is necessary, and direct measurement of success or failure for church programs cannot be accomplished as easily as using profit and/or loss in business or test score averages in education. Therefore a new measurement—one that accounts for ministry effectiveness—must be employed.

Creating new performance indicators is never perfect, but it is far superior to no evaluation at all. Appropriate ministry metrics need to be identified by each program leader and discussed with the finance committee at the time of funding. Metrics for evaluating program success might be attendance, for example, at the summer Bible camp, worship services, Sunday school, preschool, Bible study groups, or excursions. Perhaps Sunday school success could be measured more effectively by totaling the number of classes rather than simply counting attendance. The metric could also be expressed as a percentage of the membership rather than an absolute number. For instance, your goal might be 25 percent of membership participation to measure the success of a yearly church garage sale.

Ministry metrics can also be used to spur on those persons involved with community relations and publicity to, for instance, increase the number of column inches given to those activities reported in the newspaper. The metric selected should be the one that best measures the program activity being evaluated. Only your imagination will limit the development of appropriate ministry metrics.

Sometimes, however, even commonly used indicators of success must be employed carefully. For example, percentage of active membership at worship services is often used to measure the success of the worship program. Yet congregations facing changes in pastors during the year might find that such a metric is an unsatisfactory indicator until the new pastor assumes full control.

Not all activities and programs of the church, including some of the broader activities of the pastor and the general office staff, will lead themselves to this type of evaluation. Rather than inventing a contrived metric, it is more realistic to recognize that such unmeasurable activities/functions exist. In these cases, obtaining a clear statement of goals and objectives for each activity or function is the best that can be achieved.

LONG-RANGE PLANNING

Most churches are geared to establishing their plans and allocating resources for a specific calendar year or fiscal year (defined as any year except a calendar year, i.e. July 1-June 30). Almost as important is to plan even further into the future. Churches must be constantly alert to changing conditions that might alter their goals, objectives, and programs. Without such a perspective they might find themselves in financial difficulty. For instance, many urban churches failed to recognize soon enough that their constituency was changing and income sources were eroding. As a consequence, some activities were continued when they could (or should) have been dropped or scaled back. Today a large percentage of urban churches are operating at a loss and are being bailed out financially by income provided by their past investments and their denomination's central organization. However many urban churches have had to close their doors. Long-term planning might have helped.

Other churches are more fortunate and lie in the path of population growth. But here too, valuable resources and opportunities can be squandered without adequate long-term planning. For example, one Texas city's population expanded from 72,000 to 250,000 in ten years. Churches serving 100 or so members in the rural outskirts of the city were quickly transformed into churches that needed to serve thousands in bustling suburban housing tracts. Those churches that had done long-term planning and had acquired sufficient land for buildings and parking and had built with future expansion in mind thrived. Some churches, however, were not prepared for growth. They had bought and built small and found themselves continually modifying one thing or another to make do. One congregation even decided to sell their church and start all over again about ten miles away in the rural outskirts of the city.

Developing a master plan

All churches need some sort of long-term planning. One way churches can avoid the unexpected is to prepare a five-year, continuous master plan. The plan is continuous in that a new year is added as the current year is completed. A continuous five-year plan offers the advantage of forcing church officials to continually think about the future. Using this approach, preparation of a five-year plan is not just done once for the following five year period but becomes an ongoing, stabilized activity of the church's planning group.

There is no one correct way to prepare the five-year plan. A plan should, however, identify:

- the needs to be served in the future and how those differ from the needs of the current congregation,
- the goals, objectives, and programs (including building and capital improvement programs) that are likely to be needed, and
- the anticipated sources of income necessary to carry out the programs over the five-year period.

Such a plan would enable the church to develop a long-term stewardship education program that could help generate the momentum necessary for increased contributions. When planning and thinking are oriented toward one-year programs and fundraising efforts, this kind of long-term momentum never has the chance to develop.

Churches need to plan for both the short-term and the long-term. Planning is the prerequisite to and basis for budgeting. Preparation of the annual church budget without benefit of proper planning makes the budget a less valuable tool in guiding church affairs. Preparation of the annual church budget with proper planning makes the budget a vital link in the church's quest to reach its goals and objectives.

■ ACTION ITEMS ■

- ☐ Define your church's main goals and objectives.
- ☐ Begin to map out a five-year plan for your church. What are the needs that will need to be served? What programs will need to be initiated to meet these needs?
- ☐ Is your budget congruent with your mission?
- ☐ What metrics do you use to evaluate your progress?
- ☐ What sources of income are you anticipating?

4. BUDGETING

If done correctly, budgeting is a time-consuming process. It involves making numerous assumptions and getting considerable cooperation and compromise among people. Furthermore, people must frequently turn their thoughts away from immediate personal and business problems to budget, and invest countless unpaid hours in a grueling process. With all these unattractive features the questions arises, why budget? The answer is that for the vast majority of churches the benefits of sound budgeting outweigh all of the associated problems.

Although the reasons for budgeting might seem obvious, the benefits of doing so are worth listing. Here are at least ten reasons why budgeting is important for churches. Budgeting

(1) *formalizes planning.* As discussed earlier, budgets are an outgrowth of the planning process. Budgets force people to study the future so that they can develop a formal plan.

To get an idea of the benefits of a plan, imagine building a church parsonage without architectural drawings. You may erect and plaster the drywall and then discover you forgot electrical outlets and heating vents. Or the foundation might be laid and then you find out it crosses the property line. The building process would be chaotic at best. Similarly, the lack of a formal budget could lead to considerable "fire fighting" on the part of church leaders, thereby hampering the church's ability to attain its long-term goals and objectives. With a budget churches can anticipate potential problems and introduce measures to prevent or correct them. With budgeting, the operations of the church can be conducted from year to year with a minimum of distraction. The eventual outcomes of planning are direction-oriented church programs that are achieving their goals and objectives.

(2) *reduces emotion-charged discussions.* Churches operating without budgets (or with budgets that are acknowledged to be very flexible) are prone to spend their money erratically. The finance committee will hear emotional pleas for special, extra, emergency funds, and they will either have to approve the expenditure of funds, thereby reducing the funds needed for other programs, or deny the request, often an emotional act causing misunderstandings and hurt feelings. Churches that have heated monthly battles about spending their money should take a serious look at their budgeting process.

With a well-conceived yearly operating budget, programs and activities are funded prior to the start of the year, and program directors are expected to live within their budgets for the year. Truly exceptional circumstances may dictate a reexamination of a program allocation, but that should be rare. As a consequence, monthly meetings of the finance committee can be devoted to determining if the church is progressing toward meeting its goals and objectives and if the current financial situation is as anticipated. One church treasurer noted that "A good budget process means that 11 acts of war can be eliminated because one annual battle is substituted for 12 monthly skirmishes."

(3) *is a basis for performance evaluation.* If church officials are to have insight regarding the church's progress toward meeting its goals and objectives, continual evaluation of programs is necessary. Performance evaluation commonly involves the preparation of a financial report in which budgeted amounts are compared with actual spending. Variances or deviations from the budget are then highlighted. Keep in mind, however, that such an analysis only compares dollars budgeted with dollars spent. It does not show if the dollars were spent wisely. By using ministry metrics of success, as discussed earlier, program expectations can and should be contrasted with program results at the same time.

Performance should be measured against a budget for the same time period. Although the budget relies on numerous assumptions, the finance committee can adequately appraise performance if care has been exercised in the formulation of the budget and if all available information is considered.

(4) *is a basis for control and provides the necessary authorization for church officers to spend money.* By using budgets to evaluate performance, church management can exercise control. If variances from the budget—either under or over budget—are out of line, the appropriate church leaders can make inquiries and take corrective action. Corrective action might be in the form of seeking additional contributions, cutting costs, or increasing or changing personnel. Such control helps the church keep on target in terms of achieving its original plan. Control not only assists in eliminating any deviations from budgets, but it also renders valuable perspectives for the next round of the planning process. By closely monitoring church operations each month, members of the finance committee get a better feel of the church's business affairs, which in turn leads to more effective management. Also, without the approval of a formal budget, church officers are unable to disburse funds on behalf of the church. Approval of the annual budget gives leaders the ability to make fiscal decisions.

(5) *assists in communication and coordination.* A church is involved in a myriad of activities. These activities are handled by many different committees and leaders. The budget process

serves as a gigantic blender to communicate, integrate, and coordinate all of these activities in order to achieve the church's goals and objectives. Obviously, in any process where different views are represented, there must be some compromise to achieve a successful result. If each activity or program attempted to satisfy its own objectives regardless of its impact on others, the church would suffer continuous in-fighting and poor overall performance. The process of establishing a budget allows the communication that is necessary for compromise.

(6) *gets members involved*. By getting members to share their ideas, thoughts, opinions, and dreams about what activities and programs the church should sponsor, you improve the chances for program success. Comments such as, "It's their program" will turn into "It's our program." For larger congregations, it may be impractical to solicit input from the entire congregation on budgetary issues. Typically, the church board or finance committee will take on the responsibility for drafting the budget. This doesn't, however, negate the fact that churches get better buy-in and support of their members when everyone feels they have a voice in the process and are kept informed of decisions.

(7) *increases the commitment to giving*. When people have participated in the formulation of the budget, they are more apt to make sure that the budgeted results occur. Stated differently, *the stewardship commitment increases with the amount of involvement in the planning and budgeting process*. This point is often missed in churches that have highly centralized budgeting approaches. Involved, committed members are much more likely to contribute than are members who are kept distant from the financial affairs of the church but then are asked to contribute.

(8) *generates confidence in the church's leadership*. Picture the situation over at St. Chaos. Without goals and objectives, the budgeting process was a travesty. Operating in such a climate, the clergy and top-level lay leaders would need special divine guidance to be successful. Alternatively, when both long-term and short-term goals and objectives are prepared and sound budgets are established, programs are more likely to be successful. In such an environment, members of the congregation tend to take more seriously calls by the leadership for greater participation, changes, new missions, and special gifting.

> **"A good budget process means that 11 acts of war can be eliminated because one annual battle is substituted for 12 monthly skirmishes."**

(9) *allows for continued operation when cash receipts and disbursements are mismatched*. Many churches have a cash flow situation in which excess funds are available to the church for several months of the year, but the excess must be retained to cover the fixed costs of operating the church during the summer months, when attendance and giving are traditionally lower. Without appropriate budgeting, excess funds could be allocated by a finance committee after hearing an emotionally charged plea for funds. Summer bills may go unpaid; summer programs may be suspended. For churches having mismatched inflows and outflows of cash, budgeting helps to maintain financial discipline.

(10) *allows time to lend or borrow prudently*. A church's annual operating budget may show a net cash deficit or surplus for the year. If the deficit, for example, cannot be eliminated with the church's existing assets, such as the sale of securities, the church must borrow. Some churches can obtain loans from their regional or national denominational offices. Other churches borrow at a bank. Either way, budgets help to pinpoint how much money is needed and when it is needed. The situation of having a surplus of funds is more pleasant, but here, too, the budget allows the church to think through

the appropriate places to invest its excess funds. Without sufficient time to plan investments, the church is not likely to get the best available return or to understand all of the risks involved in each possible investment vehicle.

As basic as it might seem, churches don't always recognize the vital importance of preparing a budget and using it to guide its financial operations. Failure to recognize the importance of budgeting has caused many churches to experience severe financial distress. This failure has even contributed to the demise of some churches.

> **Stewardship commitment increases with the amount of involvement in the planning and budgeting process.**

POWER OF A NAME

In most organizations, leaders have years of training and experience. No such training tends to accompany the selection of people asked to serve on the committee that allocates church resources through the budgeting process. Whether the group is called the budget committee, administrative committee, board of directors, finance committee, or something else, people are typically selected on the basis of their willingness to serve and their business acumen. No training is required; no certification is necessary. As a consequence, members of these committees often do not know how to carry out their responsibilities. Thus, using common sense, members of a budget committee, for example, will determine that their job is to budget, which often means to complete a form. But no one tells them exactly how to go about the budgeting process.

Similarly, members of a finance committee will determine that their job is to monitor the church's financial situation. But, again, no one tells them precisely how to monitor the financial situation. This is like putting someone in the middle of a lacrosse field without any instructions about how the game is played. You might have had similar experiences yourself when joining a game. Remember the uncertainty you felt before someone made the rules clear to you? You might have even held up play until you were satisfied you wouldn't make a mistake.

Uncertainty

Picture the situation if no one in the game really knows the rules, and your requests for information are met with silence, stares, and shrugged shoulders. Unfortunately, many church financial committees operate just that way.

Committees who don't know how to carry out their responsibilities cause some interesting outcomes. For example, some finance committees believe that their only job is to check on the activities of the bookkeeper or treasurer. They demand extensive monthly financial reports, sometimes as long as twenty pages, which provide breakdowns of all money received and spent, by program or budget unit, in dollars and cents. They believe that their responsibility is to make certain that every penny is accounted for and recorded in the proper accounts. Obviously such finance committees need to be redirected and to start monitoring the performance of the church in meeting its goals and objectives.

Another common occurrence involves the transformation of businesspeople who are asked to serve on budget and/or finance committees. Successful local businesspeople are often appointed to these committees because tough decisions need to be made, and perhaps prior committees had difficulty making them. After all, in these situations could anyone function better than a businessperson, who routinely makes tough, "make or break" decisions?

Unfortunately no one considers that, as discussed earlier, the profit sector is clearly focused on the "bottom line," whereas the nonprofit sector has no such built-in focus. Hence businesspeople often find 1) that the church has no stated long-term or short-term goals and objectives, 2) that success in programs is either not measured or hard to measure, and 3) that the process of selecting among human needs programs is more emotional than selecting among new lines of merchandise. When this occurs a businessperson can quickly change from an action-oriented, hard-nosed decision-maker to an extremely accommodating person who can't wait to finish out his or her term of office.

Help give some direction

After working with or for churches for many decades, I have concluded that the name of the resource allocation group makes a huge difference in its effectiveness. There is power and scope in a name. You can give guidance through a name. By labeling a committee *the finance and program evaluation committee*, for example, instead of just the finance committee or budget committee, you provide members of the committee with a perspective that might not have occurred to them. You want more than programs, more than allocating funds, more than a periodic accounting of dollars spent. You want all programs continuously evaluated to make sure they are meeting their objectives. After all, only successful programs will enable the church to reach its overall goals and objectives. And if targets are reached, this reinforces the core beliefs of the congregation. The name change, therefore, is not merely cosmetic. Real changes usually result.

Some churches separate the duties of resource allocation/finance from program evaluation. This division works satisfactorily as long as both functions are being performed and both groups are kept well informed. For instance, if a program is considered unsuccessful one year, the program evaluation committee should advise the finance committee whether to reduce, eliminate, or maintain next year's appropriation of funds.

Many churches never evaluate the programs that they fund year after year. If program evaluation is made part of the committee's name, it indicates a paradigm shift that has taken place in the role of the finance committee and its members' responsibilities.

One final thought: When you're selecting members to serve on your finance committee, it's great to have experts, such as bankers, business owners, and CPAs. Don't overlook the importance of having ministry leaders on the committee, too, though. They will provide a critical perspective when it comes to evaluating programs and establishing ministry metrics.

■ ACTION ITEMS ■

- ☐ Of the ten reasons why budgeting is important, which reasons clarified the purpose of budgeting for you and your team?
- ☐ What is the name of your planning and budgeting committee? What new name might better articulate the role of this committee and energize the people involved?
- ☐ Think about your current budgeting process. What direction do you give to the committee or to your program leaders before embarking on the planning and budgeting process? What changes, if any, do you need to make to maximize the planning and budgeting process?

5. BUDGET DIRECTIONS

Budgets can be prepared in two directions: top-down or bottom-up. Each direction has important advantages and disadvantages.

TOP-DOWN APPROACH

With the top-down approach, virtually all budget development takes place at the upper echelons of the church, usually by a group handpicked by church leaders. The budget is imposed on all members of the church, who rarely become involved in the planning process. The congregation may be asked to vote on and approve the budget, but time for discussion is purposely kept short, questions may be discouraged, and the motion and second to adopt the budget are quick and often pre-selected.

Top-down approach—advantages

On paper, the top-down approach offers the advantage of sound budget preparation, reflecting all of the overall goals of the church. Preparation in this instance is carried out by those who have the best view of church operations, that is, the church leaders. Further, this approach is efficient for both budget preparers and other church members. Preparers save months by not having to debate ideas with the membership while church members are spared the difficulty of coping with financial information, program goals, and hours of debate.

Top-down approach—disadvantages

In most cases these apparent advantages give rise to a significant problem. When the budget is imposed from above, people not involved in the budgeting process often feel left out because their opinions and suggestions were not solicited. Although those in the general membership are asked to support the budget with their contributions, they are not asked to contribute their ideas. Obtaining members' involvement and financial support might be difficult. As a consequence, the top-down approach generally is met with resentment or the attitude that the budget is the property of the group that prepared it, neither of which bode well for budget adherence.

BOTTOM-UP APPROACH

Unlike the top-down approach, bottom-up budgeting centers on broad-based participation in the development process. Standing committees are asked to prepare their own budgets. Ideas for new programs are solicited, and proposed budgets are prepared. Office personnel are asked to submit their requests for new equipment and operating supplies. Teachers are asked to think about their classroom needs and submit requests. Clergy is similarly involved, as the amounts for housing, transportation, secretarial assistance, and other operating expenses must be anticipated. The idea in the bottom-up approach is to get as many people involved in the budgeting process as possible.

The bottom-up approach usually begins with the issuance of general budget guidelines, including the due dates, by church leaders or the finance and program evaluation committee (or equivalent). Written budgets and requests for funds, prepared by many different people, go to the finance and program evaluation committee for review. This group thoroughly reviews the needs for funds and invites the people and committees seeking funds to present in person their budget requests and their goals and to answer questions. Sessions are businesslike but friendly and open to all.

Budget requests are accepted, rejected, or modified by this group. The rationale for any modification or rejection is clearly stated by the committee so that everyone in attendance can understand the decision-making process. In this environment members could leave disappointed because their favorite program was not fully funded or not funded at all, but they will not leave angry because they were not heard. In its deliberations, the committee constantly points out that it must carry out its responsibility to the church as a whole, not to individual programs, activities, or people.

Bottom-up approach—advantages

The bottom-up approach is not 100 percent bottom-up; there has to be some direction and coordination from church leaders. Nevertheless, the bottom-up approach offers several distinct advantages over a budget that is handed down by church leaders with a "here it is; meet it" attitude.

First, bottom-up, participative budgets are really self-imposed. By consulting with and incorporating the opinions of a large number of the church membership, greater strides are made toward budget adherence. In other words, individual members know that their views are valued by church leaders and others. Morale and satisfaction are greater with this approach, so extensive efforts are made to meet budgetary targets.

Second, the budget is constructed by people who are close to the action and who know the ins and outs of programs and activities. The same cannot be said for a budget that is prepared in a top-down manner. The bottom-up approach usually results, therefore, in more realistic goals for both the inflows and the outflows of cash.

Bottom-up approach—disadvantages

The bottom-up approach is more time consuming and cumbersome to administer than the top-down approach because of increased member involvement. Despite these problems participative budgeting is an effective tool among progressively administered churches. Because the broad perspectives of church leaders are used in conjunction with the detailed operating knowledge of program leaders and others working within the church, a powerful budget is created, one that incorporates the views of all levels of the church hierarchy and indeed all interested members.

Let's put your understanding of budget direction approaches to the test by referring to the information for First Church.

FIRST CHURCH

Situation. First Church prepares its budget for a calendar year, January 1-December 31. It begins the annual budgeting process in late August, when the budget committee, composed of key church leaders, establishes targets for total contributions and expenditures for the next year. Built into the targets is an increase in the church's bank savings account desired by leaders to cover unexpected contingencies.

The stewardship committee is given the target for contributions and is expected to devise methods for achieving the goal. On the expenditure side, budgets for all programs, activities, and functions are developed with the targets of the budget committee kept in mind.

None of the areas has achieved its budget in recent years. Contributions typically do not meet the target. When contributions fall short, each area is expected to cut costs so that the savings objective can still be met. But the church can rarely increase its savings account because the funds have already been spent, are in the process of being spent, or cannot be cut for some unquestionable reason. In fact many costs are higher than the original budget, and the church usually has to draw on its dwindling bank account to get through the year. Church leaders, disturbed that First Church has not been able to meet its targets, are thinking of hiring a cost control consultant to rectify the problem.

Analysis. In analyzing the situation at First Church, consider first how the budgeting process employed by the church contributes to its failure to meet the targets. The budget at First Church is a top-down budget, which probably includes many unrealistic expectations and excludes the human interaction essential to an effective budgeting/control process. True participation in the preparation of the budget is minimal, limited to a perfunctory gathering and manipulation of the amounts to meet the prescribed targets. This suggests that there will be little enthusiasm for meeting the budget.

Leaders at First Church do not provide any basis for their targets, so no one knows whether the targets are realistic. But the targets anticipate a small surplus, and the church repeatedly spends more than anticipated, so perhaps the targets are unrealistic. Perhaps there is a genuine long-term financial imbalance. The church might need external assistance more immediately with fundraising rather than with cost control. On the other hand, unless the expenditure budgets are too low, the programs that continually spend more than their budgets allow are candidates for a cost review.

What should First Church do? First Church should consider the adoption of a bottom-up budget approach. All people responsible for performance under the budget would participate in the decisions by which the budget is established. Such participation includes setting goals and objectives. Although time consuming, the approach should produce a more acceptable, effective goal/control mechanism. This involvement encourages ownership of the budget and a cooperative attitude throughout the budget period. The budget becomes self-imposed not imposed by others. The dynamics involved in all members working toward common goals will greatly enhance the church's ability to meet its targets.

■ ACTION ITEMS ■

- ☐ Which budgeting approach is your church currently using—top-down or bottom-up?
- ☐ How effective has this approach been?
- ☐ What would be the pros and cons of changing to a new approach?

6. BUDGET APPROACHES

There are two approaches to preparing the church's annual operating budget: incremental budgeting and program budgeting.

INCREMENTAL BUDGETING

Incremental budgeting, often called *line item* or *traditional* budgeting, is based on the question, how much did it cost last year? Most churches follow this budgeting approach. Incremental budgeting takes this year's budget as the basis for next year's budget and makes adjustments to each item for anticipated cost or activity changes. For example, assume that the Bible school served the needs of 100 children this year at a total cost of $3,000 ($30 per child). Further assume that the Bible school anticipates serving 125 children next year and, because of inflation, the cost per student will rise to $40. Using the incremental approach, next year's budget for the Bible school will be $5,000 (125 x $40). Incremental budgeting gets its name from the fact that the budget changes incrementally from year to year. An abbreviated example of an incremental budget for a hypothetical church is presented in Example 1.2.

Flaws

The incremental approach has several points in its favor. For a preparer, it is an easy one with which to work. For a user, it is easy to understand. These two advantages are important to many churches, especially smaller ones. But the approach has three serious flaws. One flaw is that the budgeted amount is almost automatic–that is, you take the past and adjust it for the future. Little attempt is made to evaluate prior activities and costs. It is therefore conceivable that a church could be continuing its ineffective and inefficient ways from one year to the next and, curiously, be willing to pay more and more money to do so. Ineffective practices could be perpetuated. Stated differently, the incremental approach presumes that the church is already spending all of its money wisely and that no improvements are necessary for the next year. This presumption, however, is never critically examined.

The second flaw is that the approach relies on the past, which cannot be changed, rather than the future, which can be changed. Finally, traditional budgeting focuses on costs, the so-called inputs necessary to achieve church objectives, not on achievements, or outputs. If your church leaders seem fixated on costs as opposed to measuring accomplishments, the budgeting system may be the culprit.

Circumstances affect cost behavior

Another problem associated with incremental budgeting is that preparers often fail to consider that costs behave differently under different circumstances. *Variable costs* alter in direct proportion to a change in the amount of activity. Examples of variable costs are the cost of food per attendee at a church picnic, or the pastor's use of automobile fuel. More miles driven would translate into higher costs. *Fixed costs* do not change over the year. Examples are insurance and salaries. *Mixed costs,* such as those for utilities and telephone service, contain both variable and fixed elements. For example, there may be a fixed monthly charge for electricity, plus a certain number of cents per kilowatt hour. Further, the rate per kilowatt hour is likely to rise dramatically with increased use because utilities want to discourage extravagant consumption of electricity. Finally, *step costs* tend to increase in chunks. For instance, a new classroom teacher needed in the early childhood school program would cause the education budget to increase by the full amount of the salary.

As a consequence of understanding the behavior of costs, churches may be able, for example, to have more activities with no additional costs, or 40 percent more activities with a 10 percent budget increase, or 10 percent more activities with a 40 percent budget increase. It all depends how costs will behave with changes in activity level. Thus, churches considering only the rate of inflation to get from one year's budget to the next will inevitably misbudget their expenditures.

PROGRAM BUDGETING

As mentioned above, traditional budgeting focuses on individual expenditures, such as salaries, supplies, and other costs. As a result, decision-making comes down to increasing, decreasing, or eliminating individual line items. Another approach to preparing the annual church budget is *program budgeting*. With this approach costs are identified with the specific programs being carried out by the church. Significantly, each program indicates its goals and objectives prior to funding. Program budgeting operates on the premise that programs are run to achieve certain purposes, and by clearly establishing these purposes the church can improve both the use of its resources and the effectiveness of its programs. This approach to budgeting forces the church to do its planning before preparing the budget. It also is the same methodology used for Generally Accepted Accounting Principles (GAAP) Statement of Activities and Statement of Functional Expenses, which means your reports will follow these standards.

Steps for the program budgeting process

The program budgeting process begins by requiring the church to identify each program/activity it conducts and the needs each one serves. Next, each program leader examines his or her program in terms of how well it is achieving its purpose. If the leader feels improvements are needed, he or she will also provide an assessment of the benefits that would be derived from making improvements to a program, as well as any cost implications of making improvements. Finally, an estimate of the resources needed to operate the program for the next year is developed. (Churches using multiyear budgets would have data prepared for a several-year period.)

Each program leader then compiles the data into a program budget format that includes a statement on the purpose of the program, a description of the services provided, program goals and objectives, the amount of money needed, and the benefits and cost of any program change requested. In preparing the program budget, each program leader receives information on how much of the common costs of operating the church (costs that are allocated among all programs) should be included in his or her budget. The final step involves review by the finance and program evaluation committee, which evaluates the costs and benefits of each program.

Benefits of program budgeting

The benefits of program budgeting are well documented. First, program budgeting provides a better understanding of what each program is attempting to do. Also, because the purposes of each program are specified, the costs of each program can, at the end of the year, be compared with the benefits achieved. Second, this budgeting approach directs program leaders' attention to program achievement—the outputs of spending the money. Remember that traditional budgeting emphasizes the disbursement and control of expenditures, such as those for electricity, maintenance, and so on.

As a consequence, the purposes of the programs can easily be overlooked. In program budgeting, program purposes and annual goals and objectives are stated up front so they are not likely to be forgotten when program success is measured.

Program budgeting offers church members a clear picture of what their contributions are supporting and provides them with numerous opportunities to become involved in the process. Both results of the process can help generate a higher level of member support for the church's activities.

Disadvantages of program budgeting

On the negative side, program budgeting takes much more time to complete than incremental budgeting. But the extra time spent is not wasted with trivial matters. It is spent planning, establishing measurable goals and objectives, and evaluating how programs should operate. Put differently, incremental budgets can be prepared without planning; program budgeting cannot be done properly without planning. Sadly too few churches use this advanced method.

> **Incremental budgets can be prepared without planning; program budgeting cannot be done properly without planning. Sadly too few churches use this advanced method.**

An example of a program budget prepared for a youth program is shown in Example 1.3. Data from the hypothetical Oak Grove Community Church from Example 1.2 is employed and recast into a program budgeting format. The youth program, of course, is just one church program; such budgets need to be prepared for all programs. In reviewing Example 1.3, notice that costs charged to the program are 1) direct costs, or costs that are easily traceable to the youth program, such as the salary of the youth director, and 2) indirect costs, such as the pastor's salary, which are spread among several programs based on estimates of time

Example 1.2: Incremental Budget

Oak Grove Community Church
Proposed Expenditures for the Year 20X2

	20X1	20X2
Salaries		
Pastor	$54,000	$57,000
Youth Director – part time	6,000	6,000
Church Secretary	27,000	26,400
Bookkeeper – part time	12,000	12,600
Janitor – part time	18,000	18,600
	$117,000	**$120,600**
Operating Expenses		
Utilities	$15,000	$18,000
Insurance	6,000	9,000
Office Supplies	1,500	1,800
Postage	2,250	3,000
Continuing Education	2,400	7,000
Automobile Expenses – Pastor	4,500	7,000
Multimedia Equipment		4,000
Flowers	1,200	1,550
Maintenance Supplies	2,400	3,100
Miscellaneous Expenses	450	900
Van	4,500	7,500
	$40,200	**$62,850**
Christian Education		
Literature	$12,000	$10,500
Bible school	3,000	5,000
Library	900	825
Refreshments	3,000	3,300
Miscellaneous Expenses	1,200	1,000
	$20,100	**$20,625**
Youth		
Retreats – Spring and Fall	$1,500	$1,800
Convention in Springfield	1,200	1,200
Teen Club	600	3,000
	$3,300	**$6,000**
Music		
Music Materials	$6,000	$6,900
Choir Robes	1,200	
Piano Repairs	300	450
Organ Repairs	600	3,000
	$8,100	**$10,350**
Missions		
Foreign Missions	$3,000	$3,900
Galt Orphanage	10,500	15,000
	$13,500	**$18,900**
Total	***$202,200***	***$239,325***

and usage. So the pastor's salary of $57,000 must be allocated to programs based on the amount of time spent on each program.

Therefore, if the pastor spends five percent of his or her time on youth activities, $2,850 ($57,000 x five percent) of the pastor's salary is added to the youth budget. The operating expenses are similarly divided up among the various programs. For example, if the new multimedia equipment is used 10 percent of the time on teen activities, $400 ($4,000 x 10 percent) is attached to the youth budget. Vehicle use, such as the use of vans and buses, can be budgeted using estimates of cost per mile or as an estimated percentage of the total cost. Comparing the budget for youth activities prepared using the incremental approach with that using the program budgeting approach is revealing. First, the program budget includes a statement on program purpose and measurable goals and objectives, whereas the incremental approach of Example 1.2 states nothing about these critical matters. Next, users of the incremental approach are led to believe that the 20X2 budget for youth activities amounts to *either* the $6,000 total shown for the youth category *or* $12,000 if the salary of the part-time youth director is included ($6,000 + $6,000), as some members might do. Notice the confusion as the incremental budgeting approach does not organize costs by program.

Using the program approach, and by allocating relevant church costs to programs, it becomes apparent that 20X2's *total* cost for youth programs amounts to $20,565, a big difference. This amount might be more than the members of the finance and program evaluation committee want to spend. Further, the program approach directs program leaders to detail the cost of changes made to their programs. In this case increasing the size and scope of the Teen Club would cost the church $3,400. Again, church officials might not want to spend so much money. On the basis of their analysis and review, they might ask the parents of the teenagers to cover more of the program's expenses.

To review, the vast majority of churches use the traditional, incremental method of budgeting, even with all of its flaws and failings. The program budgeting approach is clearly shown to be a superior method, yet it is used infrequently.

Example 1.3: Program Budget – Youth

Oak Grove Community Church
Program Budget for the Year 20X2

1. Purpose: To involve children of church members and, in some cases, nonmembers, in activities at or sponsored by the church.

2. Objectives: The program intends to hold two retreats at Camp Lockeford in May and October, serving 25 youngsters up to age 12 on each retreat; to select and accompany four high school students to the annual Convention in Springfield; and to increase the size of the Teen Club, which meets weekly, by introducing computer games and weekend fishing, bowling, and ski trips, so that by year-end it has between eight and 20 members.

3. Amount needed:

	20X1	20X2
Youth Director	$6,000	$6,000
Pastor's time – 5 percent, est.	2,700	2,850
Church Secretary's time – 5 percent, est.	1,350	1,320
Janitor's time – 5 percent, est.	900	930
Utilities – 5 percent, est.	750	900
Insurance – 5 percent, est.	300	450
Postage – 2 percent, est.	45	60
Multimedia equipment – 10 percent, est.		400
Maintenance Supplies – 5 percent, est.	120	155
Van Expenses – 20 percent, est.	900	1,500
Retreat Expenses	1,500	1,800
Convention in Springfield	1,200	1,200
Teen Club	600	3,000
Total	**$16,365**	**$20,565**

Total funds needed in 20X2 exceed those budgeted for 20X1 by $4,200. Of this amount, $3,400 relates to the planned increase in the size and scope of the Teen Club. Details for the additional costs for teen activities are as follows:

Multimedia equipment	$400
Van Use	600
Teen Club Expenses	2,400
Total	**$3,400**

■ ACTION ITEMS ■

- ☐ Which approach to budgeting does your church currently use—incremental budgeting or program budgeting?
- ☐ How receptive do you think church leaders would be to changing the method of budgeting?
- ☐ What would be the pros and cons to using either approach for your church?

7. THE ANNUAL OPERATING BUDGET

Whether the traditional line item or program budgeting approach is used, an operating budget for the annual or fiscal year must be constructed. Anticipated inflows of resources need to be matched against anticipated outflows of resources. It is important that the annual operating budget contain details on *both* inflows and outflows of resources.

This point is often missed by many churches that fail to consider inflows of resources in their budgets. For these churches, the budget is a detailed list of anticipated expenditures by functional category (salaries, utilities, and so on) similar to that shown in Example 1.2. The rationale for omitting the inflows of resources has been expressed to me in many ways, including, "The Lord has always provided," "This congregation always digs deeper if necessary," "We don't obtain pledges," and "Pledges are unenforceable." But I don't believe a church should commit itself for expenditures, particularly those long-term in nature, without having a good handle on the anticipated inflow of resources.

Imagine yourself purchasing a house, entailing substantial monthly mortgage payments, with the understanding that the money will come from somewhere because it always has. Most of us would not make such a commitment until the funds necessary to pay for the house can be realistically anticipated from steady employment. Persons have deferred buying a house until their financial situation stabilized and/or their financial path looks clear. Yet many churches only plan for expenditures and hope for contributions and gifts. It is just good common sense that the annual operating budget should include both anticipated *inflows* and *outflows* of resources.

BUDGET ESTIMATION

By its nature a budget is a series of future estimates. These estimates should not be arrived at haphazardly. Instead, significant care should be exercised in their determination.

Normally budget estimates are based on both the past and the future. That is, historical information is often a good starting point for prediction. But any changes in the church or its community of members mean that a budget trend might change. As an example, suppose a church is attempting to budget its contributions for the year. Assume that member giving has increased steadily at the rate of four percent per year for the past five years. Should economic and membership conditions remain stable, the church would be correct in anticipating a four percent increase for the upcoming period. If, however, the town's main employer recently cut its workforce or if the church has a new pastor, this factor must be taken into account. In this situation it might be prudent to anticipate a smaller increase or even no increase in contributions for the upcoming year.

Slack

In constructing the annual operating budget, two kinds of estimation difficulties can surface. In large, well-endowed, growing churches, there might be slack. Slack is an *intentional* understatement of contributions and/or overstatement of expenses. Slack may be introduced in several ways, but typically it is an overstatement of the cost necessary to purchase, for example, a piece of equipment or to operate a program or activity. Thus, when the actual expenditure is tabulated and is found to be less than the budgeted amount, no one can criticize the program leader or administrator. In fact, he or she looks like a hero for spending less than the amount budgeted. Slack, therefore, provides some leeway for those who spend the church's money.

Slack might permeate the entire budgeting process and can perpetuate itself if people to whom funds are allocated adopt the "use it or lose it" attitude found in the government. Slack creates a difficult problem for budget makers and might be hard to correct. Slack is inherently wasteful for several reasons. First, the leeway provided program leaders and administrators allows them to be casual in their spending. Second, if actual costs are less than budgeted amounts, the church has lost an opportunity to use the funds for something else during the year. Third, monthly financial discussions could be reduced to bickering over which activity has slack that could be reallocated to those programs in real need.

Optimistic estimates

Another type of budget problem commonly occurs in churches that have experienced a gradual erosion of their membership, especially in economically challenged inner city churches and small churches located in agricultural and rural areas. The problem here is often overly optimistic estimates of yearly member giving. Many churches annually overstate their anticipated resources by 10 to 20 percent! They develop and approve a budget and, when contributions lag, programs and activities are cutback, bills are paid more slowly or are deferred to future months, and improvement projects are deferred to future years.

A finance committee meeting in this kind of church focuses on monitoring the cash balance and approving bills to be paid. Using highly optimistic (i.e. ideal) targets might have merit for one year as the church strives for the unreachable in that short time frame. But repeated annual failures and a constant battle to monitor, cut, and/or defer, will cause most church members to recognize that the budget target is fabricated, and they will not feel a commitment to help meet it. A budget needs to be attainable under normal operating conditions. Budget preparers should consider what members have given in the past and should make a realistic assessment of those active members who will support the church. Phantom members cannot be relied upon for support.

Although it is easier said than done, budget estimates should be realistic, shying away from excessive optimism or pessimism. Unrealistic assumptions defeat the purpose of budgeting.

Whether you create your budget using software included in your church's comprehensive church management system, a stand-alone budgeting program, like QuickBooks®, or even a spreadsheet program, such as Microsoft's Excel®, budgeting is more than filling out a form. It is an entire process to make sure that the church achieves its goals and objectives and that its monies are wisely spent.

THE ANNUAL BUDGETING PROCESS AND TIMETABLE

As we have discussed, good budgeting takes planning, patience, and time. Assuming the church has done its planning and has stated both long- and short-term goals and objectives, the following approach, used by the hypothetical Atherton Church, is a reasonable one for most churches.

Atherton Church uses the program budgeting approach. The budget process begins on July 1 for the next calendar year with an invitation to members to submit budget requests for programs, activities, capital improvements, and equipment. Ideas for new programs are solicited. Participation by all members is encouraged. From July through September members of the finance and program evaluation committee prepare a tentative budget by making a realistic projection of expected annual giving and anticipated expenditures, sorting through all requests and meeting with program leaders and others to discuss their specific goals, objectives, and methods of operation. In this process some items may be cut back or deferred.

In October the committee conducts its annual pledge month, requesting all members to indicate their expected giving for the next calendar year. To obtain the required commitment for funds, the tentative expenditures budget is given to the congregation to provide a reference for determining their pledges. In November, after the pledges are received, the total amount of pledges is adjusted downward by a small percentage to reflect the fact that at Atherton Church not everyone can or will honor his or her pledge. On the basis of the adjusted pledges, the tentative budget is revised and becomes the final budget. Differences between the tentative budget and the final budget are typically small and involve the addition or deletion of a few pieces of equipment. The final budget is approved by the committee in November and approved by the congregation at a general church meeting in early December.

Although the six-month timetable at Atherton may seem too long, the committee does not work forty hours a week on the budget. The committee may meet only once or twice a month. Given the normal inefficiencies, absences, and interruptions that committees often experience, six months is a good rule of thumb. Churches not allowing sufficient time for budgeting are easy to spot. They are the ones groping around in January or early February without a budget for the calendar year or the ones, like St. Chaos, preparing a budget before a football game.

Example 1.4 presents a suggested timeline for the annual budgeting process. It presents the role of the finance and program evaluation committee in each time period for a church initially adopting the program budgeting approach.

Example 1.4: A Timeline for the Annual Church Budgeting Process

Initial Program Budget

July – December	January – June	July – December
Prior to budget period ☐ Review requests for funds. ☐ Review program goals and objectives. ☐ Evaluate consistency between program and church goals and objectives. ☐ Determine methods of measuring performance (proxies). ☐ Project annual giving, perhaps with pledges. ☐ Prepare tentative budget. ☐ Fine tune tentative budget. ☐ Prepare final budget.	During the budget period ☐ Compare dollars spent against budgeted amounts. ☐ Evaluate program performance. ☐ Recommend ways to improve program results	During the budget period ☐ Compare total dollars spent against budgeted amounts. ☐ Evaluate program performance for the full year. ☐ Report on program performance: recommended changes in budget amounts, program goals and objectives, methods of measuring performance and/or program leadership. Prior to the next budget period ☐ Review current year's results, reports, etc. as available. ☐ Review requests for funds. ☐ Review program goals and objectives. ☐ Evaluate consistency between program and church goals and objectives. ☐ Determine methods of measuring performance (metrics). ☐ Project annual giving, perhaps with pledges. ☐ Prepare tentative budget. ☐ Fine tune tentative budget. ☐ Prepare final budget.

BUDGETING FOR THE INFLOW OF RESOURCES

Church treasurers often express the size of their churches by indicating the size of their budgets. You'll hear that one church has a $300,000 budget, another has an $800,000 budget, and so on. Because most churches try to remain financially viable from year to year, these statements usually mean that cash equal to the stated amount will be raised during the year and then dispensed for various purposes. The figure used typically includes only cash resources and sometimes not even all the cash anticipated for church related and church derived activities.

In order to determine the total resources entrusted to the church by its members, the operating annual budget should include all economic resources provided to the church, whether in cash or not, in any of its activities. These might include: regular offerings, restricted or designated gifts, bazaars, car washes, bake sales, bingo, special canvasses and drives, tuition from educational activities, amounts given to the pastor's discretionary fund (if such a fund exists), and the value of items donated to the church.

Full-picture budget

Because most churches focus very narrowly on member-giving (i.e. offerings of cash), they do not know the total value of the resources they actually receive. Stated differently, most churches do not know what it would cost to operate the church for a year and pay cash for all goods and services. With a full-picture financial resources budget that includes all items, church financial leaders will know that, for example, of total resources of $250,000 provided, $165,000 may come from weekly member giving, $20,000 from restricted gifts, $15,000 from funds earmarked for the pastor's discretionary fund, $40,000 from tuition at preschool and Mother's Day Out, and $10,000 for miscellaneous church activities (such as bake sales).

Using a full-picture approach, this church's operating budget would be $250,000. If only weekly giving were considered, the treasurer would claim that the church has a $165,000 budget, or only 66 percent of what the full-picture financial resources budget would show. The difference can be sizable.

WEEKLY OFFERINGS

For many churches the largest inflow of cash resources comes in the form of weekly envelope offerings, perhaps made to fulfill a yearly, monthly, or weekly pledge. Although the subject of obtaining pledges is hotly debated in many congregations, most churches find that the pledge card is a most useful device in obtaining the commitment of their members and in preparing their own budgets.

Card design

If pledge cards are used, thought should be given to their design. Most are small, provide little room for comments, may not even display the church's name or logo, and focus the member's attention solely on the pledge rather than on the broader concept of financial commitment. The instrument used to gather financial commitments should have built-in excitement, with some color, the church name and logo, and perhaps a suitable passage from Scripture. The instrument should have sufficient room for people to express their feelings about their pledges.

Some people will take this opportunity to let you know why they are supporting the church, which is valuable information. It also allows people to note why they cannot or will not make a pledge. Further, by turning the card into an instrument for financial commitment not just a yearly pledge commitment, members can be asked about whether the church is included in their wills, whether they have considered tax-deductible gifts of property to the church or to any of its ministries. Members can be invited to meet with a church representative to discuss these matters. Some churches never ask these questions and, as a consequence, lose excellent opportunities to provide for their long-term financial viability. Renaming the current pledge card the *commitment card* and redesigning its elements can enable the church to elicit greater financial support.

Another key reason for using pledge cards: Standard accounting principles require that pledges be made in order to record these anticipated revenues in church financial statements. Soliciting financial commitments from your members is a key means by which you will base your anticipated cash revenues, as well as increase follow-through from your membership in fulfilling their financial commitments to the church. If you would prefer not to include these expected funds in your financial statements, the wording on the card is critical. Consult your accountant if you would like to obtain commitments from your members without being required to record the amounts in your general ledger.

Even without considering pledges, most churches could make a fairly good estimate of expected income by preparing a graph of prior years' donations and then assessing the trend. Most churches maintain extensive statistics on member contributions. Valuable information can be gained by analyzing the contributions according to, for example, frequency of giving, marital status, and age. Example 1.5 is a summary analysis of contributions according to age.

The summary can be analyzed several different ways. One way is to relate it to the life cycle of a church. For instance, the summary reveals that members younger than 21 contributed a small portion of the church funds. But it is a healthy sign to have 144 contributors in this category. People under age 21 are the future of the church.

The number of young adults in the 21- to 40-year-old range indicates the church's ability to retain its youth into adulthood. This group is low in both absolute numbers and in contributions. Only 16.7 percent of the contributions come from givers between the ages of 21 and 40. Those in the 41- to 50-year-old and 51- to 65-year-old age groups are important to churches. These people typically provide the greatest financial support and lay leadership. In Example 1.5 more than 58 percent of total giving comes from these two age groups.

The over-65 age group also has a large number of contributors. It provides 23.3 percent of total giving. This group may also be counted on more than younger members to volunteer their services because they often have more time at their disposal. But the large number of older contributors could also indicate some future financial problems for the church as the congregation ages.

Example 1.5: Summary Analysis of General Member Contributions By Age

	No. of givers	Younger than 21	21-30	31-40	41-50	51-65	Older than 65
No. of givers (500)		144	45	35	52	117	107
Total for year ($300,000)		$5,000	$30,000	$20,000	$65,000	$110,000	$70,000
Percent of Total*		1.7%	10%	6.7%	21.7%	36.7%	23.3%
Range							
Less than $100	217	138	22	7	8	21	21
$100-499	124	4	13	16	17	36	38
$500-999	69	2	3	6	9	20	29
$1,000-1,499	35		4	3	6	15	7
$1,500-1,999	22			2	1	13	6
$2,000-2,499	2				1		1
$2,500-2,999	9		1		3	2	3
$3,000-3,499	7		2		2	2	1
$3,500-3,999	7		1		2	3	1
$4,000-4,499	1					1	
$4,500-4,999	2				2		
$5,000-5,500	5				1	4	
	500	144	45	35	52	117	107

*The sum of all percentages exceeds 100% due to rounding

Using averages to analyze contributions

There are several other ways that churches can evaluate the level of member giving. Each has an appropriate use, depending on the church's circumstances. Many churches, for instance, first compute their anticipated contributions budget. They then analyze contributions by using the average contribution per contributor. For example, using Example 1.5 data, the average contribution is $600 ($300,000/500). Although this figure is easy to compute, it can be misleading. Hefty gifts made by wealthy members are comingled with smaller gifts made by others. A rule of thumb is that 80 percent of funds will come from 20 percent of the contributors. Conversely, 20 percent of funds will be provided by 80 percent of the contributors. Churches using this approach might be well advised to calculate two averages—one average for the small number of large contributors, and one for the large number of small contributors.

Some churches use an average of giving based on the number of members in the congregation. Thus, if the church in Example 1.5 had a membership of 1,000, the average contribution would be $300 ($300,000/1,000). This figure could be used together with an estimate of the next year's membership for budgeting purposes, assuming economic conditions are stable. A problem with this approach, however, is that typically many members are inactive. Those who do not participate are not apt to give. Thus, there might not be a relationship between increased contributions and increased church membership.

Increasing contributions

Some churches compute the average income received based on the average attendance at worship services. This system has great merit because it equates contributions with involvement. The causal factor to increased giving is presumed to be increased participation in worship attendance. Sunday school participation helps too.

Other churches analyze member giving in terms of families. This is because in many churches the majority of contributions come from families. Of course, using only one group when evaluating contributions is not a comprehensive approach. In fact, because of the demographics of their congregations, many churches would find this approach inappropriate.

Giving units

Some churches analyze contributions in terms of *giving units*. A church using giving units recognizes that different members have different abilities to provide financial support. With this approach the total membership of the church is analyzed according to the number of giving units, defined, for instance, as one family including husband, wife, and children. Other members' capacities to give are compared against this reference point. Based on historical patterns of giving, the following giving units might be relevant to a particular church:

Family	1
Wife – or husband – only member	1/2
Single, employed member	3/4
Wife – or husband – only member, other spouse in another church	1/3
Retired member	1/2
College student member	1/10
Youth member	1/20

So historical data must have indicated that a wife or husband-only member will give approximately 50 percent (or 1/2) of what a family contributes. Therefore, 40 members in this category would translate into 20 giving units (40 x 1/2). Similarly, 10 college students would translate into one giving unit (10 x 1/10). With this approach, a church's membership of, say, 900 members might be reduced to 350 giving units.

The giving unit approach can be used advantageously for intradenominational comparison. With the number of members translated into a common capacity for giving, churches can be evaluated in relative terms and need not be concerned with differences in absolute size. This benefit becomes especially useful when comparing one church against another. Church A might have 2,000 members and Church B might have only 500 members. Yet by converting the memberships of both churches into giving units, many financial relationships may be comparable on a giving unit basis.

Determining giving potential

Another advantage of using this approach is that it can be used to help determine the potential of the congregation to contribute. To find this potential, the number of giving units (i.e. family-giving equivalents) is multiplied by the average family income of church members. Average family income is important because, unless there are some very large benefactors, the income of the church will mirror the income of its members. Income statistics can be obtained from government websites. Of course these statistics will be representative only if the church has a cross-section of members from the community. Hence, if Assembly United Church's congregation reflects the general community and has 100 giving units and an estimated average income per member of $60,000, total income of church members would be estimated at $6,000,000 (100 x $60,000). Based on this total, a table could be prepared like the one below. It shows what the income potential of the church is with different percentages of giving.

Total giving-unit income	$6,000,000
Giving 1%	$60,000
Giving 2%	$120,000
Giving 3%	$180,000
Giving 5%	$300,000
Giving 10%	$600,000

By using this type of analysis, financial leaders can determine the percentage of the potential cash resources that the church is currently receiving. Thus, if Assembly United Church can expect to receive only $120,000 in contributions during the year, it will be receiving only two percent of available annual resources. If this percentage is deemed insufficient to support church programs, church leaders need to think of ways to stimulate greater membership involvement and, through participation, increased giving. Perhaps a program of stewardship education would be effective also. If, however, church leaders conclude that the church is receiving amounts from its members comparable to those of other churches in the same denomination, they may decide to augment income by attempting to increase membership through a new-member drive, a household visitation program, a church visitation program, or other well-publicized activities.

RESTRICTED GIFTS

Many churches do not include restricted—or designated—gifts or offerings in their budget because the funds received must be spent according to the wishes of the donor or are collected with a special purpose in mind. They are not available for the payment of regular church expenses and are essentially "in-and-out" items. But the failure to include such restricted gifts and offerings in the budget disregards the resources provided by these church members to missions, to outreach programs, or for special items within the church. Restricted funds that are to be paid out within the year would be shown as a restricted disbursement in the expense section of the same budget. If the funds are to be disbursed in the following year, they would be shown as a restricted disbursement in the expense section of the next year's budget.

PASTOR'S DISCRETIONARY FUND

Many churches have a pastor's discretionary fund, which provides additional funds for the pastor to use as he or she sees fit. Unfortunately, churches often exclude these monetary gifts in their financial reporting, or they fail to disburse these funds properly. Either of these practices can lead to serious unintended consequences.

First, only the church, not the pastor, qualifies as a tax-exempt organization. Contrary to common belief, a gift made directly to the pastor for the discretionary fund is not tax deductible. And funds that are drawn from a pastor's discretionary account should be done so only after gaining a solid understanding of the potential tax ramifications for withdrawing money from this account and ways to reduce tax liability based on proper accounting procedures. Checks made out to the pastor should be endorsed over to the church and deposited in an account that is listed in the name of the church. The pastor can then authorize payments from this account.

Another word of caution: if funds are drawn from the pastor's discretionary fund to cover routine operating expenses, the church's expense budget will be understated. Additionally, if payments to the pastor's discretionary fund go unaccounted, financial leaders will understate member giving to the church, and the congregation will not get to share the good feeling that comes from recognizing that, as a group, they are helping to provide for the needs of the pastor and his or her causes.

For these reasons, anticipated contributions to the pastor's discretionary fund need to be budgeted as resources, and later, in the expense section of the budget, as anticipated expenditures for the pastor's discretionary use. This budgeting procedure neither discourages contributions to the pastor's discretionary fund nor influences the pastor's freedom in determining how to spend the funds. The procedure merely includes in the budget the resources provided by the membership. Thus both the inflow and the outflow of funds are shown in the budget.

Financial leaders would do well to learn more about how to account for contributions made to a pastor's discretionary fund, as well as how to spend funds from this account without your pastor incurring a tax liability. An excellent resource that covers this and many other tax-related topics is Richard Hammar's annual *Church & Clergy Tax Guide* (Your Church Resources/Christianity Today International).

DONATED SERVICES

During the year a church receives many hours of donated services from members. Many volunteers are senior citizens who have some extra time on their hands. Others are busy mothers with little time to spare. Some people donate their time because they can't contribute cash. Other people give cash as well as their time and abilities. Donated services represent valuable resources for the church. They are different from cash resources only in the form that they take. Resources are resources. All are needed. All need to be budgeted, monitored, and managed.

Keep track of donated services
Records should be maintained on donated services and periodically, people should receive thanks for their gifts of time and ability. However, do not place a cash value on the time donated as some members might inadvertently deduct this amount as a charitable contribution on their federal income tax return. The value of donated services is *not* an allowable deduction for income tax purposes, and some members could become hostile when the IRS notifies them that they owe back taxes and interest. In addition to thank you notes, a growing number of churches sponsor recognition dinners or events each year to honor volunteers.

BUDGETING FOR THE OUTFLOW OF RESOURCES

The planning, budgeting, and control of church expenditures have been discussed at several points already and will not be repeated here. In fact, the majority of the discussion dealing with incremental and program budgets concerned the outflow of resources. It is sufficient here to note that the outcome of the budgeting process should be the comparison of full-picture income with full-picture expenses for the calendar year or the fiscal year. By now you know that I will recommend that expenses expressed in the budget include more than just the expected cash disbursements necessary to operate the church. The expenses should also include the disbursement of benevolences, disbursement of restricted gifts, expenses of operating church related activities such as schools, disbursements to the pastor's discretionary fund, and the use of donated property and equipment. A sample of a full-picture, all-financial-resources budget is presented in Example 1.6.

The all-financial resources budget shows that the expected resources provided to this church total $270,000. The majority of income is expected to come in the form of cash gifts, both unrestricted and restricted, but $9,000 is anticipated to come from interest, dividends and rent; $35,000 from school tuition; $14,000 from miscellaneous activities; and $10,000 from gifts of property and equipment.

On the expenditure side the budget shows that the following funds have been earmarked: $99,000 for the pastor's ministry, $48,000 for administration, $53,000 for various programs, $20,000 for benevolences at all levels, $5,000 to pay off the church's existing debt, and $10,000 for the building fund. A contingency reserve of $3,000 is planned to cover any unexpected changes in income and expenditures. This represents only one percent of total resources, a very small percentage.

essential guide to church finances

Sometimes a preliminary budget indicates that expected expenses are in excess of expected income. Some value judgments then have to be made. Questions have to be answered regarding items such as salary increases for the pastor and other employees, the amount of the pastor's expenses (housing or housing allowance, entertainment allowance, travel reimbursement, pension, and continuing ministerial education allowance), the importance of particular programs, the financial requirements of missions, the appropriate amount to add to the building fund, the possibility of deferring some expenditures until the next year, and so on. This process of reconciling expected income and expenses is, of course, an important step in the resource allocation process because it is here that the church's operating plan for the coming year is determined. The mechanics of this reconciliation process have already been discussed.

Using savings to balance the budget

In most churches the amount of budgeted inflow of resources sets the limit on budgeted expenses. Deficit spending might be popular in Washington, D. C., but it's not popular in churches. There are some instances, however, when a budget is approved showing expected revenues less than expected expenses. A church might deliberately decide to invade its accumulated savings and spend more than it receives. This decision might be made to honor commitments and keep the church moving toward its goals and objectives. Or perhaps the church might have indications that funds equal to the shortfall will be received from denominational offices or other congregations during the year. The church should, however, attempt to attain a balanced budget as soon as possible.

Alternatively, a church could budget a surplus for the year (i.e. inflow that exceeds outflow). This might occur in well-established churches where member contributors have not yet realized, or have not yet been informed, that the church's needs have diminished. It could also happen in growth situations where spending cannot keep pace with increasing membership and/or affluence. It might also occur in congregations that anticipate major renovation work or that desire to build up a contingency fund for possible difficult economic times in the future.

Example 1.6: Community Church

Full-Picture, All-Financial-Resources Operating Budget Calendar Year 20XX

Income
Pledges	$150,000
Special offerings	10,000
Cash plate	5,000
Sunday school offerings	3,000
Communion offerings	1,000
Restricted gifts	25,000
Interest and dividend income	6,000
Rental income	3,000
School tuition – all programs	35,000
Miscellaneous activities	14,000
Gifts to the pastor's discretionary fund	8,000
Gifts of property and equipment	10,000
	$270,000

Expenditures
Pastor-related
Salary	$50,000	
Housing allowance	30,000	
Car allowance	5,000	
Education allowance	1,000	
Pension	5,000	
From discretionary funds	8,000	$99,000

Administration
Salaries	$25,000	
Supplies	4,000	
Property maintenance	6,000	
Utilities	4,000	
Insurance	3,000	
Telephone	700	
Postage	1,000	
Literature	300	
Flowers	200	
Van expenses	2,800	
Publicity	1,000	48,000

Programs
School	$40,000	
Youth	5,000	
Music	4,000	
Social concerns	2,000	
Worship	2,000	53,000

Benevolences
National	$13,000	
Local	2,000	
Foreign	5,000	20,000
For restricted gifts per donor		22,000
Reductions in expenditures from gifts of property and equipment		10,000
Debt retirement fund		5,000
Building fund		10,000
Contingency reserve		3,000
		$270,000

GAMES PEOPLE PLAY

Common ploys

Because budgeting is an exercise in human interaction and debate, some people take this opportunity to play games to get what they want from the budget. One of the games used to obtain something new is called *Foot in the Door*. Beware when you hear comments that a new program has hardly any costs. It might not cost much now, but wait until a constituency is built up.

Another game is *Getting the Pastor's Blessing*. Many members of finance committees or equivalent groups have a difficult time being objective about a proposal that is said to have the approval of the pastor. Yet the proposal may be weak on its own merits. *Implied Support* is another game. Watch for statements like, "A lot of members want this," or "They'd never tell you but the members want this." Another ruse involves comparing the church with the one down the block or with a sister church in a neighboring community. This is the *But They Do It* game. A church moving forward without defined goals and objectives could fall for such ploys.

Games are also used to keep funding for established programs and activities. One game is called *The Flood*. It involves overwhelming the finance committee with more data and materials than necessary in order to impress the members. A riskier game is the *Out of Town* ploy. Here a program leader requests an amount for the year but comments that an out of town trip prevented him or her from preparing anything formal.

Last, there's the *We've Always Done It This Way* game, which is supposed to raise the item to an almost divine level so that analysis and discussion would be distasteful. Churches operating like St. Chaos could fall prey to these games and thus allocate their resources in a particularly wasteful manner.

■ ACTION ITEMS ■

- ☐ Does your annual operating budget contain details on <u>both</u> inflows and outflows of resources?
- ☐ List all the sources of income your church receives, including restricted gifts, pastor's discretionary fund, and donated services. How does accounting for these extra sources of income affect your inflow of resources?
- ☐ What steps can you take when there is a monthly shortfall in income, and what impact will your actions have on your annual budget?

8. OTHER BUDGETS

In addition to the annual operating budget, several other budgets may be constructed to guide the church's financial affairs, including the monthly cash budget, capital spending budget, and debt retirement budget.

MONTHLY CASH BUDGET

All churches benefit from the preparation of a monthly cash budget. Rarely will the church's expected monthly cash receipts exactly match the expected monthly cash expenditures. Although cash inflow will normally equal outflow for the year taken as a whole, a different

Example 1.7: All Saints' Church Cash Budget

Cash Budget for the Months of August and September 20XX

	August	September
Beginning cash balance	$1,000	$(500)
Add cash receipts		
Envelope offerings	9,000	12,000
Loose plate offerings	1,000	1,500
Restricted gifts	3,000	3,000
Special offerings	-	3,000
Electronic transfers/Online giving	$1,000	1,000
Other	4,000	1,000
	$19,000	$21,000
Cash available for disbursements		
Pastor's salary	$1,500	$1,500
Pastor's housing allowance	1,000	1,000
Administrative expenses	6,000	4,000
Program expenses	4,000	5,000
Benevolences	2,000	2,500
Mortgage payment	1,000	1,000
Disbursed restricted gifts	3,000	3,000
Total disbursements	$18,500	$18,000
Ending cash balance	$500	$3,000

story usually surfaces when cash flow is reviewed on a month-to-month basis. There might be several months when the projected cash outflow exceeds inflow, and either savings must be reduced, bills paid late, or money borrowed. A cash budget serves to summarize a church's cash activities for the budget period.

Historical patterns

To prepare a cash budget, the church's historic pattern for giving needs to be examined. Unless dramatic changes are occurring within the church, the past pattern is a good indication of how member contributions are likely to be received in the ensuing year. For example, a church might find that monthly giving is stable every month except December, which is twice the monthly average. This pattern would be included in the cash budget by having each month except December budgeted for 1/13 of the total.

Other churches might find that giving is higher in March, April, November, and December and lower in January, February, July and August and moderate in all other months. These churches would anticipate future monthly cash contributions on the basis of historical percentages. Thus, if July typically accounted for five percent of the yearly contributions, the July budget for the ensuing year would anticipate five percent of the expected annual amount. Whatever your church's pattern, adjustments will be necessary for situations where months in the preceding calendar year had a different number of Sundays than in the budget year. In other words, if December had four Sundays in the preceding year and has five Sundays this year, this year's cash budget should take the extra Sunday into account.

Cash disbursements are also projected by using historical data, knowledge of any rate increases or inflationary factors, and due dates. Many of the church's obligations will be paid monthly. Some may be paid only quarterly or annually.

An example of a cash budget for All Saints' Church for a two-month period is presented in Example 1.7. The cash budget indicates that although the church has a small cash balance at the beginning of August and will have a larger one at the end of September, the church will nearly run out of cash in August unless certain managerial actions are taken. This is important information.

CAPITAL-SPENDING BUDGET

The capital-spending budget details the costs of renovation or building projects together with the source of funds necessary to finance the projects. This budget is prepared for the asset acquisitions that have a long-term life and a high cost. Some larger expenditures that might be included in capital-spending budgets are the construction of a new church, adding on a wing, building a parsonage, repaving the parking lot, putting on a new roof, and purchasing a van. Often churches will maintain a separate building fund to accumulate funds for such large expenditures. In Example 1.6 we saw that Community Church earmarked $10,000 of current income for its building fund. Assuming that this church was planning to spend $100,000 to modernize its structure, its capital spending budget might look like Example 1.8.

As you can see from Example 1.8, the church is relying on outside financing for $48,000, or less than half of the cost of the project because internally generated funds have been accumulated for the modernization. Churches that sell bonds and solicit special building fund pledges to finance their large spending projects would include the anticipated receipt of such funds as sources of income in the capital-spending budget.

Example 1.8: Community Church

Capital-Spending Budget for the Building Modernization Project
Calendar Year 20XX

Uses of funds	
Building construction contract	$100,000
Architectural fees	1,000
Licenses, legal fees, and so on	1,500
Landscaping	1,500
Furniture and equipment	10,000
Carpeting	4,000
Total	**$118,000**

Sources of funds	
Building fund balance – beginning of the year	$58,000
From current income	10,000
From interest on building fund	2,000
From mortgage financing	48,000
Total	**$118,000**

DEBT RETIREMENT BUDGET

The debt retirement budget is used to show how the church's long-term debt will be paid off. Separate budgets could be prepared for each of the church's long-term debts, or a unified budget could be prepared for all long-term payables. As some mortgages are amortized over a thirty-year period, this budget could project thirty years into the future. Let's assume that the church took out a 12 year loan to pay for the modernization project. Churches often have a debt retirement fund, which accumulates cash for eventual disbursement to creditors. For instance, in Example 1.6, we saw that the Community Church allocated $5,000 of its current income for the debt retirement fund.

Assuming that Community Church will pay off its $48,000 mortgage by making 12 end-of-the-year payments of $5,000 for principal and interest, its debt retirement budget would appear as shown in Example 1.9. A review of this example reveals the Community Church expects to pay the first year's obligation with current income, the second year's with a special pledge drive, and the last year's with memorial gifts.

SOME OBSERVATIONS

The administering of a planning and budgeting system is a difficult task. Too often, financial people become overly involved with the mechanical aspects of budget construction. They lose sight of the fact that budgets are for their church, a voluntary group of members sharing common religious beliefs, rather than for a business corporation. Unless the budgeting effort considers human relations, even the most precise efforts will be for naught if met with resistance, skepticism, or indifference.

Be flexible
Along the same lines, many churches overemphasize the use of budgets to control expenditures. A budget is not carved in stone. A few changes in the annual operating budget or any other budget during the year might have to be made because of unanticipated events. These changes do not damage the planning and budgeting process. They simply reflect the difficulty of accurately forecasting the future.

Be realistic
As we have discussed, plans and budgets are only as effective as the effort that has gone into their preparation. Church leaders must thoroughly support the planning and budgeting processes or the entire resource allocation exercise will be a lesson in futility. Also, though planning and budgeting are crucial to a church's financial well-being, they cannot replace effective week-to-week management. Plans and budgets cannot by themselves change the course of a faltering church. They are but tools to be used by skillful leaders.

■ ACTION ITEMS ■
- ☐ Identify historical patterns for your church's monthly cash budget. What patterns emerge?
- ☐ How can you adapt to the ebb and flow of giving when faced with fixed expenses?
- ☐ How much of your current cash budget is allocated to capital spending and debt retirement?

9. STRUCTURE FOR CHANGE

The preceding material has covered the essentials of church planning and budgeting. At this point you might be one of a tiny group of people bursting with pride because of the exemplary manner in which your church does its planning and budgeting. Your church might be one of the handful of churches that needs no improvement. If this is the case, I share your joy. Clearly your church has, among other attributes, 1) definitive short-term and long-term goals, 2) programs that can be objectively measured for success, 3) member involvement in the budget process, and 4) timely, knowledgeably prepared budgets.

For most readers, however, the preceding material has exposed a variety of planning and budgeting challenges in their churches. Some deficiencies may be minor; others may need a long-term commitment to address.

For example, many readers would probably state that their church handles its resource allocation/budgeting process imperfectly, but somehow the church manages to muddle through year after year. Further, changing this process is not an easy task considering the church politics involved. So though changes might hold benefits for the church, the reality is that it will take a lot of time and effort.

Identify and categorize deficiencies

Nonetheless, the first step in improving your church's planning and budgeting process is to identify and categorize deficiencies. The format presented in Examples 1.10 and 1.11 can be used to clarify the first step. Problems are assigned 'easy to correct' or 'difficult to correct' categories for minor and major deficiencies. Obviously the analysis of deficiencies by type is critical. I advocate this approach not just because it's the model used by management consultants, but because I want you to be successful in making improvements in your church's planning and budgeting process. Early success in correcting the important deficiencies that are also relatively easy to fix will boost your self-confidence and the confidence others have in you. You will find it easier to suggest and then implement some of the more difficult changes when you have already met with some success.

The purpose in investing time and money in reading this text is to prepare you to help your church. Realize that the change agent is you, not your pastor, not another member of the congregation. Effective church planning and budgeting comes from people who want to be effective. You are in the best position to influence improvement and change. After all, you have just prepared a comprehensive deficiency list for your church's planning and budgeting process! Share your concerns; share your wisdom; share your enthusiasm. Your church will benefit from your efforts.

> ■ **ACTION ITEMS** ■
>
> ☐ How receptive do you think your church staff will be to hearing your perspective on strengths and deficiencies in your church's planning and budgeting process? What pushback might you experience?
>
> ☐ What can you do to prepare for resistance to making changes in the planning and budgeting process?

Example 1.9: Community Church

Debt Retirement Budget for the Building Modernization Project 20XX-20XX

	YEAR 1	YEAR 2	....	YEAR 12
Use of funds			....	
Mortgage payments including interest	$5,000	$5,000	....	$5,000
			....	
			....	
Source of funds				
Current income	$5,000	___	....	___
Special pledges	___	$5,000	....	___
Memorial gifts	___	___	....	$5,000
			....	
			....	
			....	
Total	$5,000	$5,000	....	$5,000

Example 1.10: The Church's Minor Deficiencies in Planning and Budgeting

	Easy to Correct	Difficult to Correct
1.		
2.		
3.		
4.		
5.		
6.		
7.		
8.		
9.		
10.		

Example 1.11: The Church's Important Deficiencies in Planning and Budgeting

	The Church's Important Deficiencies in Planning and Budgeting	
	Easy to Correct	Difficult to Correct
1.		
2.		
3.		
4.		
5.		
6.		
7.		
8.		
9.		
10.		

Chapter

Performance Measurements

by Vonna Laue

1. HOW ARE YOU DOING?

Remember the budget meeting that took place at St. Chaos Church in Chapter One? In his haste to adjourn the meeting, the finance administrator let many budget expenditures slip under the radar that never should have been approved. Now, nearing the end of its fiscal year, St. Chaos finds itself with a significant budget shortfall in several areas. Giving has dropped with the major downturn in the economy, and bills for capital improvements, like the new roof, ran over budget, forcing St. Chaos to shift money from one budget column to another, effectively robbing Peter to pay Paul. Faced with mounting pressure to provide adequate resources to the ministries whose budgets he approved, the finance administrator is wondering what to do to respond to this financial crisis. He wonders why the budget isn't working out this year. Are other churches in his area as hard hit as St. Chaos?

Unfortunately, St. Chaos isn't alone in the crisis they face. Many churches create a budget and try to run the church by the numbers. As long as the checkbook balances each month, the finance administrator must be doing a good job, right?

Actually, there are several ways for a church to measure its performance. Balancing expenses against contributions is just one way. There are several other performance measurements that financial managers can use to more accurately gauge the ministry effectiveness of their church. It is simply not enough to manage the church by whether there is cash in the bank or not.

How well are you stewarding your church's resources? How does your church compare with similar churches? What should you monitor and how? These are questions you probably wonder about but may not know how to find the answers to. In this chapter, we'll explore various measurements and ratios to help assess the health of your church, and some areas where improvements could be made.

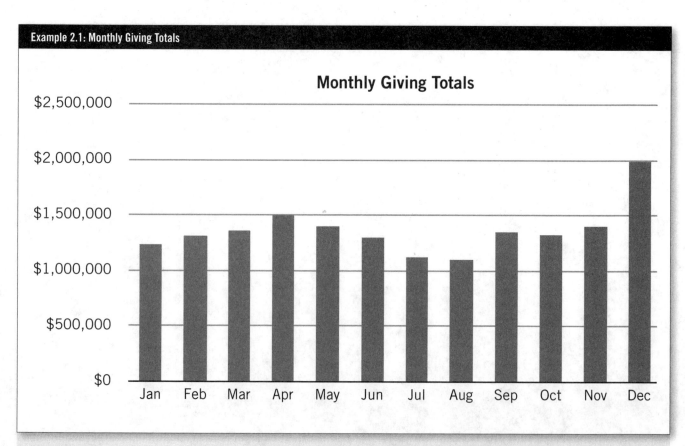

Example 2.1: Monthly Giving Totals

essential guide to church finances

There are two ways of comparing your church's financial strength and struggles. The first is within the organization itself. Inward comparisons look at financial data from prior years compared to the current year, or from budget to actual. Tracking historical trends in ratios may also be an indicator of underlying changes within your organization. This is discussed below. The other method of comparison is an outward comparison—looking at the financial information of your church against other similar sized churches. This is discussed in the Comparative Ratio and Peer Group Comparisons sections of this chapter. Let's start by considering the types of inward comparisons you can use to measure your church's overall financial performance.

2. INWARD COMPARISONS— A PLACE TO START

Sample monthly giving report and five-year comparison

A monthly giving report can provide a useful snapshot of the fluctuations in giving that a church can anticipate in the course of a year. If the financial committee at St. Chaos had been performing this type of inward comparison, it might have realized much sooner that the roof project should have been deferred until the second quarter when giving is historically higher. Understanding trends in your membership's giving may give you reason enough to consider adopting electronic funds transfers. Providing a means for people to tithe consistently helps to even out the seasonal dips in giving, such as during slower summer months when fewer people attend services. Monthly giving reports also provide a

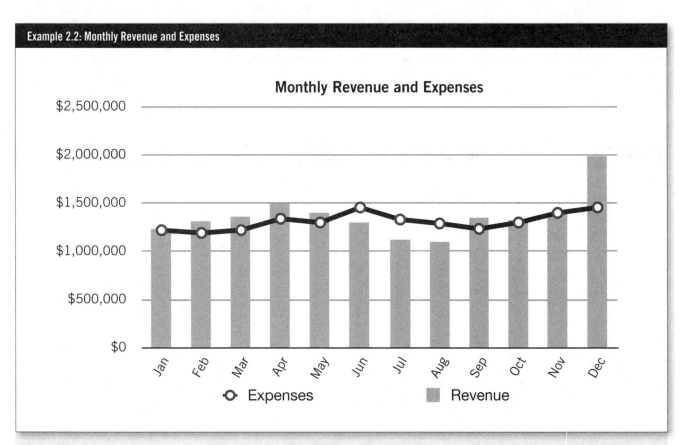

Example 2.2: Monthly Revenue and Expenses

more realistic cash forecast, which is critical to know when you're preparing the annual budget. Having this information in a graph format may be useful as well.

Example 2.1 gives a picture of the income pattern of a church. Understanding when cash shortages may exist provides opportunity to plan some purchases during different times of the year, or obtain a line of credit to help smooth the "peak and valley" effect. For example, Sunday school curriculum may be purchased in June or July to prepare for the upcoming year.

Example 2.2 shows monthly revenue and expenses together, which gives a visual of the gaps and surpluses in funding.

A year-to-year comparison may also be helpful. If your church is growing and has a consistent pattern of increased giving, that is helpful to know. If there is continual decline in giving, wishful budgeting will not create funds. You need to have a realistic view of actual giving. It may also highlight anomalies. In Example 2.3, the graph on the left shows an annual increase of approximately seven percent. The graph on the right reflects growth in year two but with a significant decline in year three due to the senior pastor's retirement and then renewed growth of approximately seven percent. The difference between the two scenarios is 20 percent, a significant differential in annual contributions for the five year period.

IMPORTANT NOTE: If you are conducting a similar analysis for your church, be sure to exclude donor restricted gifts and other one-time contributions from this analysis or show them separately. Those funds can distort the results and provide an inaccurate basis for budgeting and decision-making. While restricted funds are important, as noted in Chapter 1, it is probably most beneficial to exclude them from this analysis because they aren't recurring.

Trend analysis can also be performed by line item. You may find it useful to prepare a statement of activities, or income statements, with multiple years displayed side-by-side. Looking at individual contributions and expense lines in this way can be beneficial for budgeting purposes. It will allow you to see the funds that are received and spent over a period of time, ensuring that the spending patterns of the church align with its mission and vision.

Your church may also find it beneficial to track the trends and possibly graph the information of non-financial information. This could include worship attendance, small group attendance, baptisms, or spiritual decisions. Look at the goals of your church. Which outcomes are important to track?

Looking inward
Certain inward comparisons may be required by organizations outside of the church as well. Capital campaign consultants, for example, would be interested

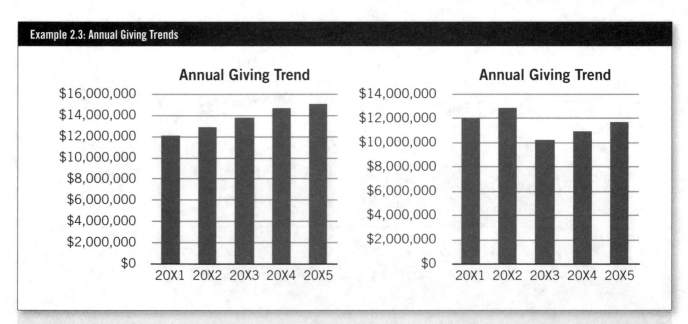

Example 2.3: Annual Giving Trends

in attendance and giving data. Lenders may also have reporting requirements related to debt covenants, or they may request some of these types of information before extending credit to your church.

You should also consider tracking the average salaries and benefits per full-time employee. (A different comparison might be necessary if you have a significant number of part-time employees). Monitoring this over time will help you determine the reasonableness of salaries as well as the changes in benefit costs to the church. If you choose to do this, you may consider separating the calculation for church employees and school employees. School employees work a more limited schedule and have a defined pay structure that varies from most church staff positions, which makes a separate analysis beneficial.

In Example 2.4 below, Church A decided to participate in a benchmarking study including other churches in their local geographic area to see how their salaries and benefits per full time employee compared to their peers. By analyzing the data below, we can see that the average and mid-point amounts are close together. This tells us that most churches in the study were close to those amounts. It also tells us that the churches at the high and low points of the range are *not typical* of the churches participating in the benchmarking study. Can you see how important this information is for Church A, which represents the maximum in the range of salaries and is almost at the maximum in the range for benefits? As you will note, comparing the salaries and benefits of their church personnel to the same information from peer churches provided them with critical information to make future salary decisions.

In the *Compensation Handbook for Church Staff* (Your Church Resources/Christianity Today International), you can review information related to various positions such as senior pastors, youth pastors, business administrators, and many more. The average salaries are provided based on key indicators including worship attendance, church income, region, and five other criteria. It's a simple way to look up comparative salary *and* benefit information.

Benefits are important for employees, especially when salaries may not be as competitive as you would like.

However, being aware of the costs and the trends related to benefits may drive you to pursue alternatives or at least research different options. Typical benefit costs that you may want to track include:

- Health insurance
- Dental insurance
- Life insurance
- Vision insurance
- Retirement contributions (403(b) or 401(k) plans, denominational plans, etc.)
- Health savings account contributions

3. COMPARATIVE RATIOS—HOW DO WE MEASURE UP AGAINST OTHER CHURCHES?

If you're ready to go beyond the internal comparisons and start looking more broadly at your church's financial performance, comparative ratios are the next step. Ratios can be a key indicator of how well a church is functioning in comparison to its peers. Not only is the actual ratio important, but also understanding how it fits in the range of peers and which churches are included as "peers."

Comparative ratios

If your financial information is compared to your peers', it may be helpful to calculate both the average (mean) and the mid-point (median). The benefit of calculating both the mean and median is to reveal the spread of results in the range. If both the mean and median are numbers that are close together, then most of the ratio results in the range are close together and the average is likely to be very useful. If the mean and median are far apart, then the underlying organizations' results are spread out and the average is less important.

An individual that works with church ratios extensively finds it useful to show a minimum and maximum in each range. This lets you know how close you are to the top or bottom of the range. Depending on the ratio observed (for example, average salary per full time equivalent), it may be beneficial to know how close to the high or low your church is in the particular range.

Another key to properly interpreting the ratios is to understand the demographics of the other participants in the range, beyond the minimum and maximum in the range. It is important to consider how many participants are in the ratio averages your church is using as a benchmark. An average ratio calculated with only a few churches may be much different than one calculated with several churches.

It is also important to benchmark your church against others similar in size and region of the country. For example, property and equipment per full time equivalent employee may be significantly different for churches in the Midwest than ones on the West Coast due to higher property costs in the West.

Benchmarking against organizations with similar asset sizes may be very misleading because organizations with older properties tend to have smaller property and equipment values due to depreciated property values. Perhaps a better way to group peer organizations is by arranging organizations together that have a similar average number of attendees (excluding children), or by the size of unrestricted charitable contributions.

There are various ways to benchmark your church against other churches. You may do it informally yourself or opt to get outside information. Several specialized studies, such as the annual *Compensation Handbook for Church Staff* by this publisher, are readily

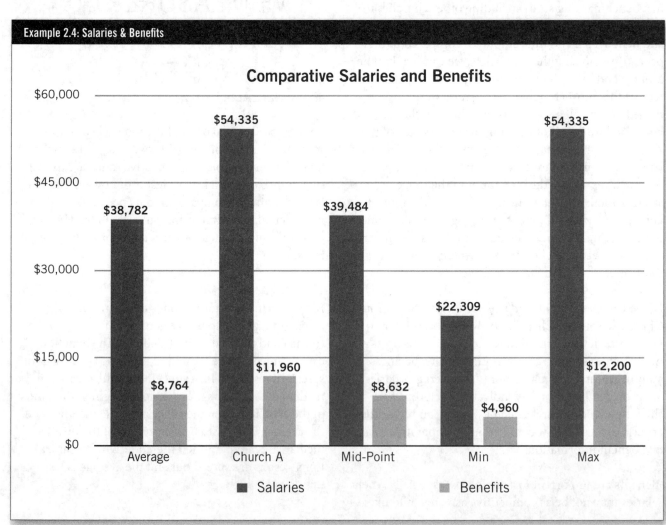

available. There is also access to more comprehensive ratio analyses. Finally, you may be able to obtain ratio information from your accountant or auditor. You would likely pay for the ratio analysis, but the easy access to information from organizations similar to yours can be very beneficial.

Once you have found your appropriate "peer group," it's time to see how your organization stacks up. With so many areas to benchmark, what are the key ratios that tell churches how they are operating or other important information and trends? Let's look at some standard comparisons and at the end of the chapter, we'll look at some additional ratios that may be helpful as well.

4. PEER GROUP COMPARISON

Sample financial statements for three churches are included in Example 2.6 through 2.11. This information is used to present peer information in this section of the chapter. The sample churches represent different sized churches and likely include a wider range of budgets than you would include in a peer group for your church. This was done to reflect the range of ratios that will result from varying sized organizations.

RATIOS BASED ON THE STATEMENT OF FINANCIAL POSITION

Included in the statement of financial position, or balance sheet, are the assets and liabilities of the church along with net assets, which are the difference between assets and liabilities. The net assets include unrestricted funds (available for operations, amounts invested in property and equipment, and board designated funds), temporarily restricted funds, and permanently restricted funds. You are obviously concerned about items such as cash and long-term debt. Below are some ratios related to the statement of financial position with descriptions of the ratio and how it is used.

Cash Availability Report: While this is not a ratio, it may be the most important tool you give to the leadership of your church. Many churches today find that senior management (pastoral staff) and the governing board want to know how much cash the church has. The most important question is not "How much do we have?" The most important question is "How much can we spend?" Typically, these are two very different answers.

> **The most important question is not "How much do we have?" The most important question is "How much can we spend?" Typically, these are two very different answers.**

A cash availability report factors in the immediate (i.e., less than 10 days) requirements related to cash to tell others what money is available to spend. It is a simple report that you can generate on a spreadsheet and provide on a monthly basis with other reports that you prepare. St. Chaos may have had a report that looked similar to this:

Cash balance as of (month end date)	$ 750,000
Accounts payable currently due	(105,000)
Upcoming payroll	(100,000)
Upcoming debt payment	(35,000)
Temporarily restricted balances	(320,000)
Available cash	$ 190,000

While temporarily restricted net assets are not a legal liability or obligation of the church, the funds are not to be expended for general operations purposes and are excluded from the cash balance for that reason. Some churches have in essence "borrowed" from temporarily restricted because they overspent from operations. This report will help you avoid these types of issues.

You will notice in this example that the cash balance was $750,000. However, the available cash was only

$190,000. Significantly different decisions will be made based on the two numbers. Providing this information to the decision-makers in your church is crucial.

Now for some ratios:

Current Ratio: This ratio helps to determine how easily the church can meet its current obligations.

$$\text{Current Ratio} = \frac{\text{Current assets}}{\text{Current liabilities}}$$

Current assets are those assets that will be converted to cash or used up within one year. Current liabilities are obligations that will be paid within one year. The current ratio relates these two amounts.

There are differences of opinion as to what the ratio results should be. In a for-profit organization, the suggested results would be 1.0-2.0. However, it is important in a church setting to remember the temporarily restricted category of net assets. Below are the current ratios for each of the sample churches.

$$\text{Church A -} \quad \frac{\$2{,}091{,}446}{\$1{,}055{,}874} = 1.98$$

$$\text{Church A - with temporarily restricted} \quad \frac{\$2{,}091{,}446}{\$1{,}055{,}874 + \$206{,}006} = 1.66$$

$$\text{Church B -} \quad \frac{\$4{,}278{,}391}{\$3{,}947{,}220} = 1.08$$

$$\text{Church B - with temporarily restricted} \quad \frac{\$4{,}278{,}391}{\$3{,}947{,}220 + \$645{,}500} = .93$$

$$\text{Church C -} \quad \frac{\$471{,}807}{\$115{,}261} = 4.09$$

$$\text{Church C - with temporarily restricted} \quad \frac{\$471{,}807}{\$115{,}261 + \$235} = 4.09$$

As you can see, smaller churches may experience a wider range of ratios. It is suggested that you include temporarily restricted net assets when computing this ratio, and then a ratio range of 1.0-2.0 would appear reasonable. A ratio of less than 1.0 reflects that the church does not have enough current assets to pay its upcoming liabilities. In this case, a church might need to borrow from restricted funds or obtain a temporary line of credit to cover short-term obligations. You want to be aware of this and monitor the ratio on an ongoing basis to keep from being surprised by a cash shortage.

Debt-to-Net Assets Ratio: This ratio considers the amount of debt a church has incurred and carries as related to the net assets, or equity, of the entire organization. This ratio shows how the assets included on the statement of financial position are "financed." The larger the ratio, the more the church owes to debt financing. The lower the ratio, the more the church owns and holds without debt obligations. While there is no pre-determined "perfect" range, the leadership in your church will need to determine the comfort level they would like to operate within related to external and internal financing.

$$\text{Debt-to-Net Assets Ratio} = \frac{\text{Total long-term debt (including current portion)}}{\text{Total net assets}}$$

$$\text{Church A -} \quad \frac{\$9{,}000{,}401}{\$13{,}361{,}238} = .67$$

$$\text{Church B -} \quad \frac{\$13{,}648{,}299}{\$11{,}890{,}658} = 1.15$$

$$\text{Church C -} \quad \frac{\$4{,}314{,}696}{\$2{,}143{,}116} = 2.01$$

Debt-to-Fixed Assets Ratio: This ratio considers how much of your fixed assets (property, buildings, and equipment) are financed.

> **IMPORTANT NOTE:** Keep in mind that fixed assets are always recorded and carried in your financial statements at the original cost less any related accumulated depreciation. This can be difficult to understand. It seems unreasonable that land purchased forty years ago for $25,000 and that is currently worth $1,500,000 would still be included

for the original purchase price. The accounting standards require this treatment. It may result in additional discussion when the financial statements or these ratios are reviewed.

Depreciation is another factor that can be troublesome to many. Nonprofit organizations are not required to pay taxes and therefore many individuals feel it is unnecessary to track depreciation. Again, the accounting standards require it. However, if a church begins to budget depreciation into their annual budgets and set those funds aside for a reserve, it can serve a useful purpose.

Depreciation should be calculated over the "useful life" of the asset. If an HVAC system with a cost of $150,000 is expected to last 15 years, the depreciation recorded each year would be $10,000. If those same funds were budgeted and reserved by the church, money would be available to replace the unit after that time period. This can be very beneficial for large items. Many churches get surprised by these unbudgeted, large-dollar replacements and sometimes find it necessary to obtain financing options in order to maintain the necessary upkeep of the facilities.

$$\text{Debt-to-Fixed Assets Ratio} = \frac{\text{Total long-term debt (including current portion)}}{\text{Total fixed assets}}$$

$$\text{Church A -} \quad \frac{\$9,000,401}{\$20,461,414} = .44$$

$$\text{Church B -} \quad \frac{\$13,648,299}{\$24,319,791} = .56$$

$$\text{Church C -} \quad \frac{\$4,314,696}{\$6,006,426} = .72$$

Debt Per Attendee Ratio: Each church will need to determine the level of debt that they are comfortable with. There will be varying opinions within congregations. Some people believe that a church should not incur debt while others are very comfortable with a high debt load. This ratio of dividing total debt by the number of attendees will vary based on the philosophy of the church. In the review of financial information from several churches, an average amount of debt per attendee was $2,500. There is no specific target amount. Some churches are very debt averse and will not obtain outside financing at all. Other churches feel like they should use whatever options are available to them to provide ministry to the community. This ratio helps to analyze the amount of debt between churches better than just comparing the total amount of debt. It may be the most useful when considering whether new debt should be incurred or not.

RATIOS BASED ON THE STATEMENT OF ACTIVITIES

Providing your congregation with information from the statement of activity is a good way to engage members in the finances of the church without preaching a tithing sermon. Some pastors are reluctant to ask for money from the pulpit. Yet if people are not aware of the needs of the church and the costs associated with the services and benefits provided, they may have very little incentive to help.

An update in the bulletin on a weekly, monthly, or quarterly basis can provide the necessary information to help congregants make an informed decision about their giving. This would typically include the actual contributions receiving for that time frame, the budgeted giving for the same period, and the budget and actual expenses as well. Here is a sample of the information that could be included:

> The board approved budgeted contributions for the year are $1,754,191 with budgeted expenses of $1,683,845. We have included a comparison of actual to budgeted amounts below for your review. If you have any questions, please feel free to contact the church office.
>
> Budgeted contributions through June 30: $867,327
> Actual contributions through June 30: $763,492
>
> Budgeted expenses through June 30: $ 826,833
> Actual expenses through June 30: $ 762,619
>
> Total budget overage/(shortage): $ (39,621)

! IMPORTANT NOTE: All of the calculations and ratios mentioned in this section should consider only unrestricted contributions unless otherwise noted. As discussed before, temporarily restricted contributions are designated by donors to be used for specific purposes and cannot be used for the ongoing operations of the church.

Contributions Per Attendee or Per Family Unit: Consider providing the congregation with the contribution per attendee or family unit information. This calculation can also be compared from year-to-year to see the trends and determine the impact on the church and the budget. Even consider calculating what contributions would be if every family made a certain amount (i.e. $50,000/year) and tithed on that amount. You could make the congregation aware of what the current giving is and what the projected giving would be if everyone participated.

Salaries as a Percentage of Contributions and Expenses: The largest expense on the financial statements of most churches will be salaries and benefits. You are not in the business of selling products or manufacturing items. You provide services and these services are performed by individuals, some of which you pay and some of which are provided by volunteers. It is understandable that this expense is greater than the other expenses you incur. If you are challenged because of the amount of salaries you provide, it may be helpful to understand the ratios related to these expenses especially as related to your peers.

We will look at two ratios. The first is salaries as a percentage of contributions and the second is salaries as a percentage of expenses. These percentages will typically differ significantly only if there are substantial inflow streams besides contributions, such as ministry program revenue or auxiliary services such as school tuition or bookstore sales that result in additional expenses.

Salaries and Benefits/Unrestricted Contributions Example:

$$\text{Church A -} \quad \frac{\$5{,}429{,}253}{\$11{,}948{,}743} = 45\%$$

$$\text{Church B -} \quad \frac{\$6{,}554{,}247}{\$17{,}294{,}593} = 38\%$$

$$\text{Church C -} \quad \frac{\$685{,}461}{\$1{,}412{,}279} = 49\%$$

Salaries and Benefits/Expenses Example:

$$\text{Church A -} \quad \frac{\$5{,}429{,}253}{\$12{,}653{,}463} = 43\%$$

$$\text{Church B -} \quad \frac{\$6{,}554{,}247}{\$24{,}666{,}532} = 27\%$$

$$\text{Church C -} \quad \frac{\$685{,}461}{\$1{,}745{,}979} = 39\%$$

The lower percentages noted above for Church B are the result of the church having significant expenses related to a media ministry. These types of ministries are very expensive and will increase expenses without a corresponding increase in salaries and benefits. It is expected that many churches will have ratios in the 40 to 50 percent range for personnel costs.

Debt Service and Debt Coverage Ratios: There are other statement of activity ratios that relate to debt similar to the ratios discussed in the statement of financial position portion of this chapter. The ratios discussed here pertain more to the debt service (payment requirements of the debt), whereas the ratios discussed previously related more to the amount of total debt of the church.

The first ratio is the debt service ratio. This ratio looks at the percentage of contributions that will be used to make the annual debt payments. A sample of the calculations are reflected below.

$$\text{Debt Service Ratio} = \frac{\text{Annual required principal and interest payments}}{\text{Unrestricted contributions}}$$

$$\text{Church A -} \quad \frac{\$805,255}{\$11,948,743} = 7\%$$

$$\text{Church B -} \quad \frac{\$1,173,368}{\$17,294,593} = 7\%$$

$$\text{Church C -} \quad \frac{\$207,178}{\$1,412,279} = 15\%$$

$$\text{Debt Coverage Ratio} = \frac{\text{Unrestricted change in net assets + principal and interest + depreciation}}{\text{Principal and interest}}$$

$$\text{Church A -} \quad \frac{\$1,402,299 + \$805,255 + \$782,913}{\$805,255} = 3.7$$

$$\text{Church B -} \quad \frac{\$1,932,734 + \$1,173,368 + \$1,530,693}{\$1,173,368} = 4.0$$

$$\text{Church A -} \quad \frac{\$66,113 + \$207,178 + \$217,643}{\$207,178} = 2.4$$

This ratio is used to determine how many times a church would be able to cover its current annual debt obligations from current operations. This may factor in to the amount of reserves the church leadership may deem to be necessary.

Operating Ratio: Finally in this section, we will discuss the operating ratio. The unrestricted change in assets (similar to net income or net loss in the profit sector) is a measure of operational results for management. The temporarily restricted change in net assets is only a matter of timing. Restricted gifts are given and may be used in that year or in a subsequent year. Management accepts the donor's designation when they accept the gift and will spend it when the time is appropriate. The change in unrestricted net assets more closely explains whether management met the anticipated targets for spending. The operating ratio defines what percentage of unrestricted revenues resulted in an operating margin. The opposite way of viewing this ratio is what percentage of revenues was spent during the year.

$$\text{Operating Ratio} = \frac{\text{Unrestricted change in net assets}}{\text{Unrestricted revenues}}$$

$$\text{Church A -} \quad \frac{\$1,402,299}{\$14,055,762} = 10\%$$

$$\text{Church B -} \quad \frac{\$1,932,734}{\$26,599,266} = 7\%$$

$$\text{Church C -} \quad \frac{\$66,113}{\$1,812,092} = 4\%$$

Churches may not want to have large surpluses every year. They may want to make sure that money is invested in the ministries of the church. They will want to make sure some reserves are in place, and monitoring this ratio and its trend from year to year will help determine the financial health of an organization. For example, the church may build reserves for a few years to launch a new ministry or a satellite campus. Then for a year or two there will be significant net losses as that ministry begins operation. If the positive years had not happened first, the ministry launch may not have been possible.

Look at Example 2.5, which reflects the positive change in net assets (net income) over a seven year period. It includes a few years of surplus with a couple of years of "investment," followed by a stabilization of income. The average of those years is included on the graph as well to show how the surpluses and deficits averaged for the period shown.

The key to any performance measurement is to find what works best for your church and is helpful in having the numbers support the ministry and not drive it. What is the mission of your church? What do you need to measure to determine the effectiveness? Can the finances reflect some degree of success or failure in those purposes? Begin to view the numbers and the people who work with them as support to accomplish the church's calling.

Ministries should annually review whether the performance measurements they are using are adequate and necessary. You may find that you need additional analysis in some areas. Perhaps you'll discover that what was once a helpful ratio, no longer provides useful information or creates unnecessary work.

The ratios previously discussed are some of the more common or useful ones that churches employ. Following are some additional ratios you may consider using. The end of this chapter also includes a sample monthly monitoring report (Example 2.12) and a sample annual monitoring report. (Example 2.13).

ADDITIONAL RATIOS

Church bookstores

If your church has a bookstore operation, but you're not exactly sure if it's meeting your ministry objectives, you may find the following ratios helpful. If your church has other operations that require keeping inventory on hand, you may want to prepare these ratios for each operation separately, and then determine a total sales and inventory ratio for all inventory-based operations in your church.

Gross Profit Margin Ratio:

$$\text{Gross Profit Margin Ratio} = \frac{(\text{Net sales revenue} - \text{cost of goods sold})}{\text{Net sales revenue}}$$

$$\text{Church B -} \frac{\$2,572,179 - \$1,222,117}{\$2,572,179} = 52\%$$

The gross profit margin ratio shows the mark-up that has been earned on the sale of church-related books and materials. This is a ratio that is most helpful when used in a trend analysis. Gross profit margins that are tracked over time help churches identify when there are unusual variances. Causes for variances may include:

1. More or less favorable purchasing arrangements
2. Inventory obsolescence issues – if there is more inventory being written off, the gross profit margin will decrease
3. Changes in markup percentages

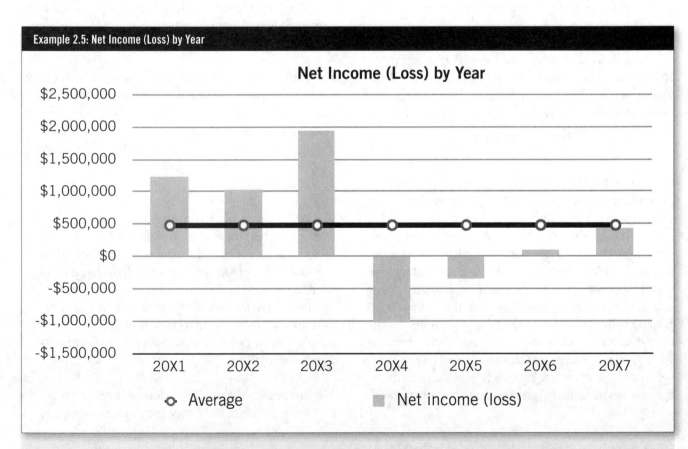

Example 2.5: Net Income (Loss) by Year

Days of Inventory on Hand Calculation:

$$\text{Days of Inventory on Hand} = \frac{\text{Inventory balance}}{(\text{Cost of goods sold}/365)}$$

$$\text{Church B -} \quad \frac{\$889{,}603}{(\$1{,}222{,}117/365)} = 266 \text{ days}$$

Many prefer to use 260 days rather than 365 because they will not be shipping on weekends. As a church, you may decide to divide cost of goods sold by 52 because that is how many Sundays the bookstore will be open. Monitoring the days of inventory on hand helps to determine how much storage space is necessary and if the inventory could be reduced to a level that would require less space. As this ratio is monitored, you will be able to also determine if excess inventory is being held. If the number of days on hand continues to increase, it is likely that obsolete inventory is being held and should be written off and given away or sold at a reduced price.

Inventory Turnover Calculation:

$$\text{Inventory Turnover} = \frac{\text{Cost of goods sold}}{\text{Average inventory ((beginning inventory + ending inventory)/2)}}$$

$$\text{Church B -} \quad \frac{\$1{,}222{,}117}{(\$877{,}864+\$889{,}603)/2} = 1.4 \text{ turns}$$

This ratio notes how many times inventory is sold and replaced in a year on average. It is preferable for this number to increase over time, indicating that you are keeping smaller amounts of inventory on hand and simply replacing it more often. If you are able to purchase a large amount of a product for a significantly reduced price, these results will be distorted. That is often the case when a pastor or other staff member is involved in the production of an item such as a book. The publisher will provide a large quantity to the individual, or the ministry they are associated with, for a drastically reduced price. Maintaining these quantities will reflect much lower inventory turns than if you had not purchased the large amount.

This ratio can also be calculated by major category of inventory. The benefit of doing this is that it helps to segregate which items are turning or moving more quickly and which items are not. This can be useful in determining if an item needs to be written off for obsolescence. While it is not possible to calculate inventory turns for every item in inventory, it is useful if calculated for significant products or categories of inventory and provided to the bookstore manager on an interim basis.

Quick Ratio:

$$\text{Quick Ratio} = \frac{\text{Current assets} - \text{inventory}}{\text{Current liabilities (consider including temporarily restricted net assets)}}$$

The quick ratio is very similar to the current ratio. It simply excludes inventory from current assets. This will not significantly impact most church operations unless they have a large bookstore operation or something similar. The reason this is helpful for churches with significant inventory is because they cannot liquidate the inventory easily if they need the funds to pay bills. This ratio gives a more accurate picture of the availability of assets to cover current obligations. The quick ratio for Church B would look like this:

$$\text{Church B -} \quad \frac{\$4{,}278{,}391 - \$889{,}603}{\$3{,}947{,}220} = .86$$

$$\text{Church B - with temporarily restricted} \quad \frac{\$4{,}278{,}391 - \$889{,}603}{\$3{,}947{,}220 + \$645{,}500} = .74$$

For Church B the ratio reflects less liquidity than the current ratio calculated earlier. Management would want to be careful to determine that they were monitoring cash flow carefully and possibly preparing cash projections to plan for upcoming expenses. This organization is large enough that they may also want to consider the use of a line of credit with their financial institution to cover certain times of the year.

General Operations

Cash Reserve Ratio:

$$\text{Cash Reserve Ratio} = \frac{\text{Cash}}{(\text{Total expenses}/12)}$$

The title of this ratio is not formally recognized. However, it will show the number of months of cash on hand as related to expenses. As noted earlier in this chapter, some churches will desire to maintain a certain amount of reserves. The reserves can be used for economic downturns or unexpected expenses or events. Often, churches that try to build up reserves will have a goal of three months (reflected in the ratio at 3.0). The months of expenses on hand for the sample churches are reflected here:

$$\text{Church A} - \frac{\$1,820,981}{\$12,653,463/12} = 1.73$$

$$\text{Church B} - \frac{\$2,959,306}{\$24,666,532/12} = 1.44$$

$$\text{Church C} - \frac{\$409,514}{\$1,745,979/12} = 2.81$$

Salaries and Debt Service to Expenses Ratio:

$$\text{Salaries and Debt Service to Expenses Ratio} = \frac{\text{Salaries and benefits} + \text{annual principal and interest}}{\text{Total expenses}}$$

This ratio allows you to look at two of the largest expenses of the church and determine the portion of the operating budget that will be utilized. Often, a growth cycle will result in an amount of debt that you anticipate being able to pay off as more people are able and encouraged to attend. However, you need to be able to pay the bills and provide the services that will attract new people with the current budget. Reviewing this calculation in advance of any major debt decisions will help analyze the possibility of the facility expansion goals.

$$\text{Church A} - \frac{\$5,429,253 + \$805,255}{\$12,653,463} = 49\%$$

$$\text{Church B} - \frac{\$6,554,247 + \$1,173,368}{\$24,666,532} = 31\%$$

$$\text{Church C} - \frac{\$685,461 + \$207,178}{\$1,745,979} = 51\%$$

Facilities Expense to Total Expense Ratio:

$$\text{Facilities Expenses to Total Expenses Ratio} = \frac{\text{Facilities expenses}}{\text{Total expenses}}$$

Facilities expense ratios can vary whether the church has new or older facilities. They may also rent rather than own. There are many churches that have taken the position to meet in community venues such as local schools and invest the money that would have been used for facilities back into ministry. These decisions will impact the ratios. You can determine whether you want to compare with other churches or just benchmark your church against itself.

$$\text{Church A} - \frac{\$1,509,253}{\$12,653,463} = 12\%$$

$$\text{Church B} - \frac{\$1,718,192}{\$24,666,532} = 7\%$$

$$\text{Church C} - \frac{\$158,758}{\$1,745,979} = 9\%$$

Missions Expense to Total Expense Ratio:

$$\text{Missions Expenses to Total Expenses Ratio} = \frac{\text{Missions expenses}}{\text{Total expenses}}$$

Missions expenses are handled differently by different congregations. Your church may determine that they want to tithe off of the offerings received. You can see in the calculations of the sample churches that they use their funds for things other than direct missions costs. The support of missionary-type activities is all that is included in the following ratios. Your church may participate in missions trips and other types of outreach activities that you would include in this ratio as well. Your church may also decide that the ministries they provide are very important and these ministries should be the focus of budgeted expenses. Whatever the decision is, these types of ratios can help leadership determine if funds are being spent as they had planned.

Church A - $\dfrac{\$221{,}883}{\$12{,}653{,}463} = 1.8\%$

Church B - $\dfrac{\$78{,}801}{\$24{,}666{,}532} = 0.3\%$

Church C - $\dfrac{\$49{,}513}{\$1{,}745{,}979} = 2.8\%$

Ministry Expense to Total Expense Ratio:

$$\text{Ministry Expenses to Total Expenses Ratio} = \dfrac{\text{Direct ministry expenses}}{\text{Total expenses}}$$

This ratio is similar to the previous missions ratio. It looks at the amount of funds expended on ministry purposes as compared to total expenses. When there are economic difficulties in a church, ministry and mission expenses are usually the first to be decreased. The debt service payments are not discretionary and personnel costs are difficult to reduce. Monitoring this ratio over several years will allow you to monitor if the percentages change over time.

Church A - $\dfrac{\$2{,}291{,}284}{\$12{,}653{,}463} = 18\%$

Church B - $\dfrac{\$4{,}124{,}234}{\$24{,}666{,}532} = 17\%$

Church C - $\dfrac{\$165{,}658}{\$1{,}745{,}979} = 9\%$

Restricted Funds to Total Contributions Ratio:

$$\text{Restricted Funds to Total Contributions Ratio} = \dfrac{\text{Restricted contributions}}{\text{Total contributions}}$$

Church A - $\dfrac{\$163{,}170}{\$12{,}111{,}913} = 1.3\%$

Church B - $\dfrac{\$2{,}753{,}889}{\$20{,}048{,}812} = 13.7\%$

Church C - $\dfrac{\$5{,}879}{\$1{,}418{,}158} = 0.4\%$

Today, churches have to look at contributions differently than at any time in the past. Generational differences are very strong even in the way people contribute to their church. Young people tend to give to specific purposes and projects and be less interested in giving to general operations. This creates budgeting concerns.

One church has begun to find ways to "market" operating projects. They established a repairs and replacement fund. As the church has needs, they make the congregation aware of the need in the bulletin. When the project is completed, they give updates including pictures of the repairs or replacements. This personalizes it more and helps to raise funds for necessary items and use the giving habits of the generations to serve the needs of the church.

Churches that receive large amounts of donor restricted contributions should consider adopting a gift acceptance policy. Such a policy would include what type of gifts would be received (cash, stock, etc.). It could also include what donor designated amounts the church will accept. If the church is never going to buy a pipe organ for example, there is no reason to accept funds for such a purpose.

Return on Net Asset Ratio:

$$\text{Return on Net Assets Ratio} = \dfrac{\text{Total change in net assets (net income or net loss)}}{\text{Total net assets at the beginning of the year}}$$

Church A - $\dfrac{\$1{,}518{,}187}{\$11{,}843{,}051} = 12.8\%$

Church B - $\dfrac{\$957{,}583}{\$10{,}933{,}075} = 8.8\%$

Church C - $\dfrac{\$55{,}581}{\$2{,}087{,}535} = 2.7\%$

This ratio indicates the total economic return on net assets. A decline in this ratio may be appropriate if it reflects strategy to better fulfill the church's mission. An improving trend indicates that the church is increasing its net assets and is likely to be able to set aside financial resources to strengthen its future financial flexibility.

Facility Cost Per Square Foot: You may also want to consider this as a potentially helpful ratio. If comparing yourself to peers with this ratio, make sure that you are comparing to other churches that have a campus that is similar in age. The costs may vary significantly if one campus is seven years old and the other is seventy.

Information Technology Ratios: With the increase in technology in the church environment, more and more people are beginning to ask what portion of the budget should be allocated to these costs. Some will look at the information technology cost per square foot (against peers) and some will look at it as a percentage of expenses. Technology experts are concerned when the percentage is below three percent of total expenses. However, you will likely find that many churches spend less than one percent. Generally speaking, newer churches spend more on technology and use it as a means of outreach.

If your church has not used any ratio analysis, now is a good time to start. Don't try to start by using all of the options given above. Choose a couple that align closely with your mission and goals and begin to examine them and possibly find peers that you can benchmark from as well. Also, remember that these are a sampling of ratios that are available to you. Most of the basic ratios necessary to help with your church's operations are included. However, you need to measure what is important to your goals. If that's not included here, you can research other ratios or develop your own to track changes over time. The key is to begin somewhere and adjust as necessary to help your church be as successful as possible.

If you are a church business administrator, here are some steps you can take to get started:

☐ Prepare a monthly analysis of the key ratios and trends for the leadership team. Format this presentation so that the key ratios are summarized in a top report or "dashboard" presentation to appropriately direct the leadership's team attention. Supplement this dashboard report by providing a more detailed financial analysis as part of your overall monthly reporting package.
☐ Consider including information periodically in the bulletin or other communication pieces to the congregation.
☐ Prepare an annual analysis of the church's financial health and trends.

If you are a senior pastor, work with the business administrator to determine the appropriate measurements that reflect the financial position of the church. Carefully review the information your business administrator prepares and support him or her by conveying to the staff the importance of this information.

For audit committees and board of directors, you can help measure the financial effectiveness of your church by:

☐ letting the business administrator know what information is helpful to you in making significant financial decisions and monitoring the financial situation of the church, and
☐ providing ongoing feedback on the usefulness of the trend reports provided. Each piece of information requires a certain amount of work. If you won't be using it, let them know. They can save the time or use it to do something that is more beneficial for you.

■ ACTION ITEMS ■

☐ Review the strategic goals of the church, and assess the financial goals set by the leadership. What ratios will be helpful to communicate the finances of the church?
☐ What ratios indicate important information for future decisions?
☐ Consider which churches you might ask to serve as peers to each other, and explore what information would be beneficial to share to help establish meaningful benchmarks for your church.

Example 2.6: Sample Financial Statement

Church A

Statement of Financial Position
December 31, 20XX

ASSETS:

Current assets:

Cash and cash equivalents	$1,820,981
Accounts receivables, net	37,511
Prepaid expenses and other assets	232,954
	2,091,446
Restricted cash	480,000
Notes receivable	125,000
Land, buildings, and equipment - at cost, net	20,461,414
Total Assets	**$23,157,860**

LIABILITIES AND NET ASSETS:

Current liabilities:

Accounts payable	$303,004
Accrued expenses	417,062
Deferred revenue	76,155
Notes payable - current portion	259,653
	1,055,874
Notes payable - net of current portion	8,740,748
	9,796,622

Net assets:

Unrestricted:

Undesignated	1,694,219
Net investment in land, buildings, and equipment	11,461,013
Total unrestricted net assets	13,155,232
Temporarily restricted	206,006
Total net assets	**13,361,238**
Total Liabilities and Net Assets	**$23,157,860**

Example 2.7: Sample Financial Statement

Church A

Statement of Activities
For the Year Ended December 31, 20XX

	Unrestricted	Temporarily Restricted	Total
SUPPORT, REVENUE, AND RECLASSIFICATIONS:			
Contributions	$ 11,948,743	$163,170	$ 12,111,913
Program revenue	2,033,071	-	2,033,071
Investment income	26,666	-	26,666
Net assets released from restrictions:			
Missions, church plant, and other projects	47,282	(47,282)	-
Total Support, Revenue, and Reclassifications	14,055,762	115,888	14,171,650
EXPENSES:			
Program services			
Church ministries and programs	9,335,359	-	9,335,359
Supporting services			
General and administration	2,816,210	-	2,816,210
Fundraising	501,894	-	501,894
Total Expenses	12,653,463	-	12,653,463
Change in Net Assets	1,402,299	115,888	1,518,187
Net Assets, Beginning of Year	11,752,933	90,118	11,843,051
Net Assets, End of Year	$ 13,155,232	$ 206,006	$ 13,361,238

Included in expenses above:	
Debt service	$805,255
Depreciation expense	$782,913
Facilities expense	$1,509,253
Missions expense	$221,883
Direct ministry expense	$2,291,284
Salaries and benefits	$5,429,253

Example 2.8: Sample Financial Statement

Church B
Statement of Financial Position
December 31, 20XX

ASSETS:

Current assets:

Cash and cash equivalents	$2,959,306
Investments	36,404
Inventory	889,603
Receivables, net	293,655
Prepaid expenses and other assets	99,423
	4,278,391
Receivable	45,736
Deferred debt issue costs	54,129
Assets held for rabbi trust	118,978
Land, buildings, and equipment - at cost, net	24,319,791

Total Assets — **$28,817,025**

LIABILITIES AND NET ASSETS:

Current liabilities:

Accounts payable	$2,266,090
Accrued expenses	468,919
Deferred revenue	424,081
Rabbi trust liability	118,978
Debt - current portion	669,152
	3,947,220
Debt - net of current portion	12,979,147
	16,926,367

Net assets:

Unrestricted:

Undesignated	573,666
Net investment in land, buildings, and equipment	10,671,492
Total unrestricted net assets	11,245,158
Temporarily restricted	645,500

Total net assets — 11,890,658

Total Liabilities and Net Assets — **$28,817,025**

Example 2.9: Sample Financial Statement

Church B
Statement of Activities
For the Year Ended December 31, 20XX

	Unrestricted	Temporarily Restricted	Total
SUPPORT, REVENUE, AND RECLASSIFICATIONS:			
Contributions	$17,294,593	$2,753,889	$20,048,812
Program revenue	1,088,077	–	1,088,077
Tuition and fees	1,738,522	–	1,738,522
Sales income	2,572,179	–	2,572,179
Investment income	95,713	–	95,713
Other income	81,182	–	81,182
Net assets released from restrictions:			
Missions, church plant, and other projects	3,729,040	(3,729,040)	–
Total Support, Revenue, and Reclassifications	26,599,266	(975,151)	25,624,115
EXPENSES:			
Program services			
Church ministries and programs	22,978,808	–	22,978,808
Supporting services			
General and administration	1,516,383	–	1,516,383
Fundraising	171,341	–	171,341
Total Expenses	24,666,532	–	24,666,532
Change in Net Assets	1,932,734	(975,151)	957,583
Net Assets, Beginning of Year	9,312,424	1,612,651	10,933,075
Net Assets, End of Year	$11,245,158	$645,500	$11,890,658

Included in expenses above:	
Debt service	$1,173,368
Depreciation expense	$1,530,693
Facilities expense	$1,718,192
Missions expense	$78,801
Direct ministry expense	$4,124,234
Salaries and benefits	$6,554,247

Example 2.10: Sample Financial Statement

Church C

Statement of Financial Position
December 31, 20XX

ASSETS:

Current assets:		
	Cash and cash equivalents	$409,514
	Inventory	54,798
	Prepaid expenses and other assets	7,495
		471,807
	Land, buildings, and equipment - at cost, net	6,006,426
Total Assets		**$6,478,233**

LIABILITIES AND NET ASSETS:

Current liabilities:		
	Accounts payable	$9,266
	Accrued expenses	11,155
	Notes payable - current portion	94,840
		115,261
	Notes payable - net of current position	4,219,856
		4,335,117
Net assets:		
	Unrestricted:	
	Undesignated	451,151
	Net investment in land, buildings, and equipment	1,691,730
	Total unrestricted net assets	2,142,881
	Temporarily restricted	235
Total net assets		2,143,116
Total Liabilities and Net Assets		**$6,478,233**

Example 2.11: Sample Financial Statement

Church C

Statement of Activities
For the Year Ended December 31, 20XX

	Unrestricted	Temporarily Restricted	Total
SUPPORT, REVENUE, AND RECLASSIFICATIONS:			
Contributions	$1,412,279	$5,879	$1,418,158
Tuition and fees	100,035	–	100,035
Program revenue	216,688	–	216,688
Sales income	63,227	–	63,227
Other income	3,452	–	3,452
Net assets released from restrictions:			
Missions, church plant, and other projects	16,411	(16,411)	–
Total Support, Revenue, and Reclassifications	1,812,092	(10,532)	1,801,560
EXPENSES:			
Program services			
Church ministries and programs	1,437,310	–	1,437,310
Supporting services			
General and administration	308,669	–	308,669
Fundraising	–	–	–
Total Expenses	1,745,979	–	1,745,979
Change in Net Assets	66,113	(10,532)	55,581
Net Assets, Beginning of Year	2,076,678	10,767	2,087,535
Net Assets, End of Year	$2,142,881	$235	$2,143,116
Included in expenses above:			
Debt service	$207,178		
Depreciation expense	$217,643		
Facilities expense	$158,758		
Missions expense	$49,513		
Direct ministry expense	$165,658		
Salaries and benefits	$685,461		

Example 2.12: Sample Monthly Monitoring Report

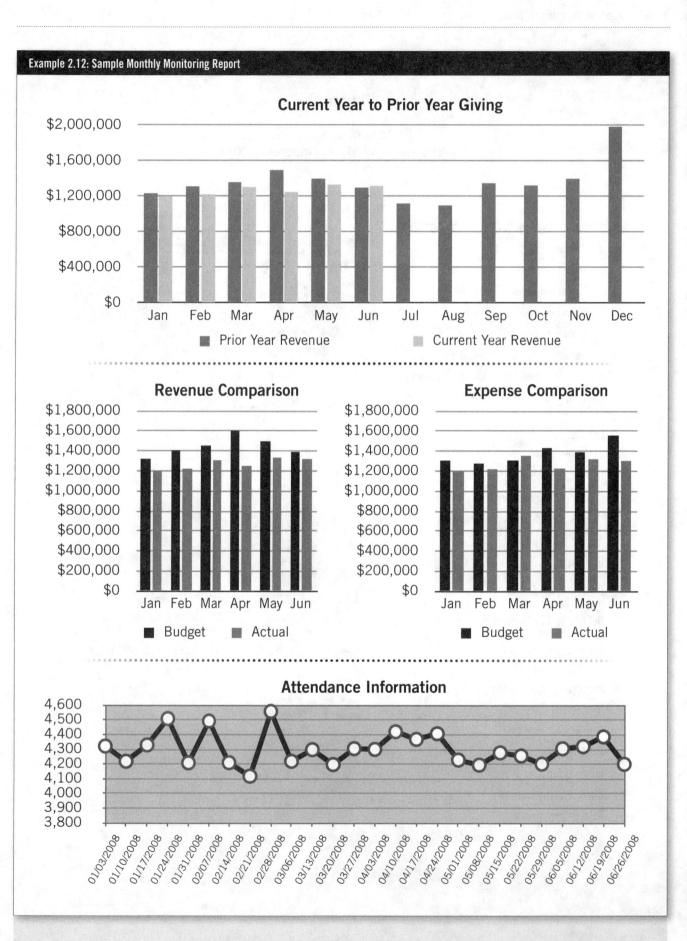

essential guide to church finances

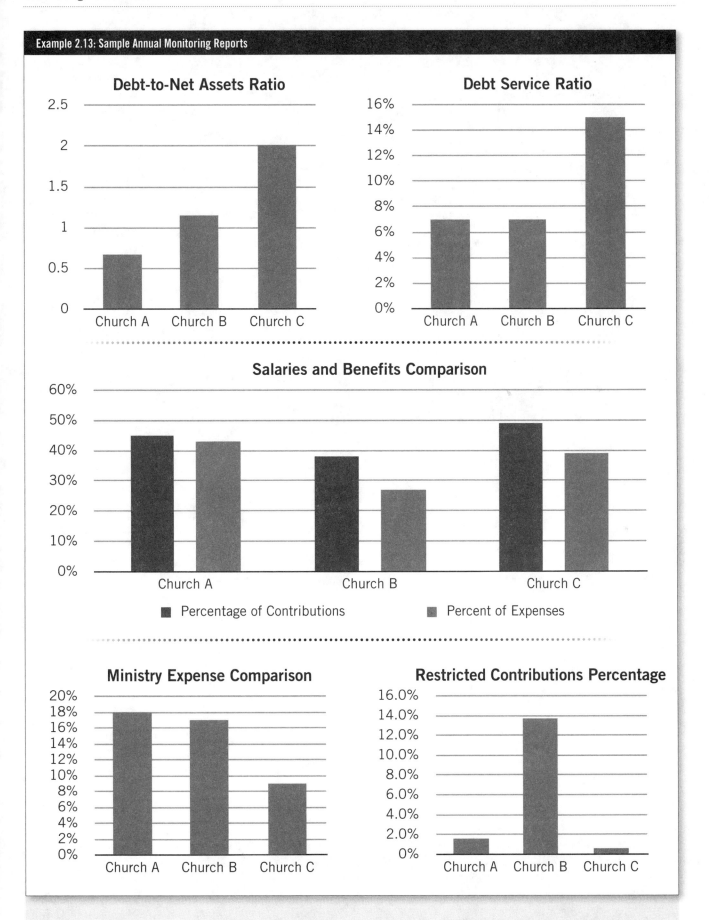

Example 2.13: Sample Annual Monitoring Reports

61

Chapter 3

Church Financial Reporting

by Richard J. Vargo

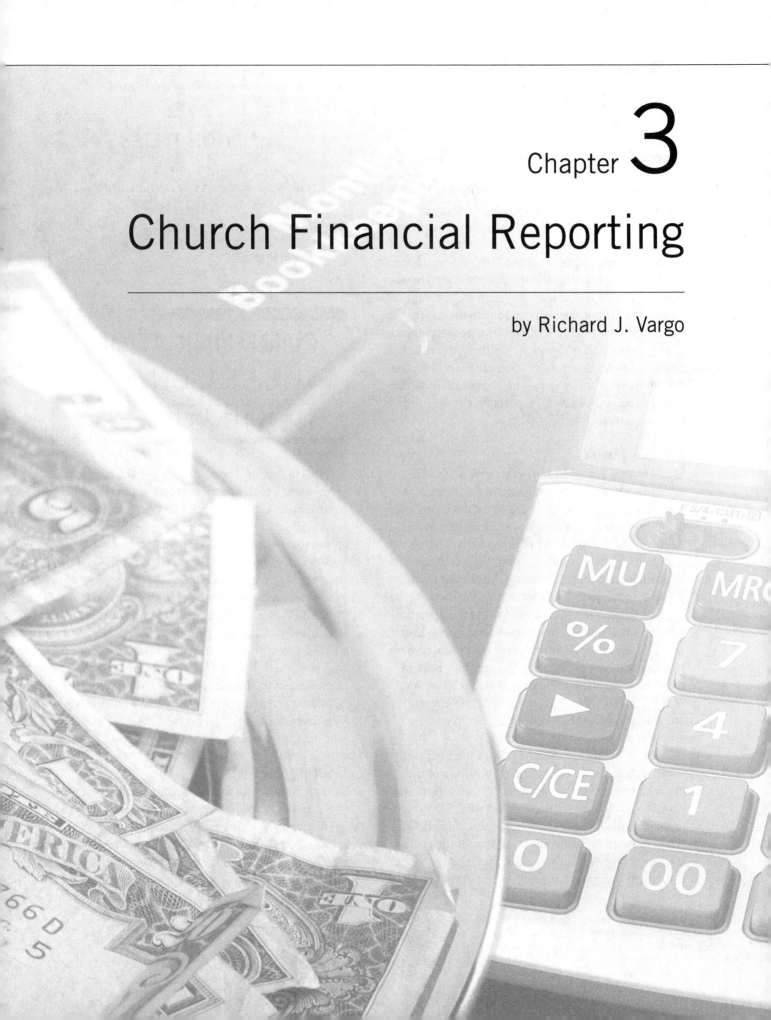

1. EFFECTIVE FINANCIAL REPORTING

Financial statements are the end products of the accounting process. You don't budget for the sake of budgeting, or process data for the sake of accounting. You do this preparatory work to ensure that users of church financial reports receive information relevant to their needs. Budgeting and the processing of transactions through the accounting system are not ends in themselves. All of this work is done to make sure that the church financial reports can be used for planning, control, and decision making. Similarly, the ratios we discussed in the previous chapter are useful because they give you information—information that can be used to create meaningful reports for the decision-makers in your church.

Unclear reports

Without well-prepared financial reports, church administrators may misunderstand (or disregard) the financial data and make incorrect decisions. New programs may be approved, raises may be granted, and debt may be incurred—all in error. Many church accountants make it a point to attend all meetings where their financial reports are being distributed just to prevent such events from occurring. Further, because the financial reports distributed to the congregation are often unintelligible to many members, many churches fail to receive the full financial support of their membership. Statements such as, "Why do they have to make these financial statements so difficult to understand?" and "What good are financial statements if no one understands them?" are common.

Because many members can't rely on the financial statements to assess the financial condition of the church, they must rely on someone else's interpretation. If a church leader they respect says, "The financial reports shows that the church is in financial difficulty," it will have quite a different effect than if the same statement comes from someone who is not respected. Frustrated members can't help but hold back some of their support. Full financial support comes from members who understand the financial reports.

■ ACTION ITEMS ■

☐ Review samples of financial reports you currently produce for your church.

☐ What do you think the strengths and weaknesses of each report are for finance committee members, board members, and congregants?

2. COMMUNICATION: THE REASON TO REPORT

The key to financial reporting by the church treasurer is to remember that reports are issued to communicate information. Communication is the process of sending information and receiving a response. For communication to be effective, a channel must be established between the sender and the receiver through which a message is sent and a response is received. An appropriate response indicates both that the message was clear and that the receiver understood the message. Breakdowns in communication occur if the sender fails to send a clear message, the receiver fails to understand the message, or both problems occur. In most churches the failure of the financial reports to communicate can be attributed to problems with both the sender (the treasurer) and the receivers (the finance committee, administrative board, or membership).

Sending problems

In regard to the treasurer's situation, first, there's the problem of tradition. If certain financial reports have been issued monthly for eons, most treasurers are reluctant to change the reporting format. After all, they may hold the position for only a year and not feel sufficiently confident to second guess their predecessors.

Second, there's the problem of knowledge. Many church treasurers who are pressed into service do not have an accounting background. Thus although they hear receiver complaints, they don't know what to do about them.

Third, there's the problem of feedback. Some receivers do not complain because if they are too critical of the financial reports, they might end up being next year's treasurer. Thus, receiver complaints are often muted or hidden.

Fourth, a treasurer might often have a misplaced emphasis. He or she might spend countless hours processing every transaction through 400 different accounts and subaccounts, balancing "the books" to the penny. This treasurer feels that his or her role is to process data not communicate financial information, and that the role of the receiver is to validate his or her work. This attitude results in financial reports that are voluminous, complex, and perhaps incomprehensible—but correct. The financial statements might be presented the same way a proud artist presents a piece of art.

Receiving problems

There are also problems on the receiving end. Members of the administrative board or finance committee, for example, might be selected because they can help the church face the financial challenges of the year ahead. Some might be astute business people. Yet these people can become unnerved quickly when they try to read the church's financial reports and realize that they are not familiar with church accounting methods. They might be accustomed to the accrual basis of accounting, used in the profit sector; the church probably uses the cash basis, used in the nonprofit sector. They might never have seen fund accounting, transfers between funds, pledges, or noncash contributions in their businesses. This lack of expertise in nonprofit accounting might render the financial reports less useful than they would otherwise be. Stated differently, the message might not be fully received.

Members of the general congregation have the same kind of problem. But here the problem is magnified because many members have not previously received and understood financial information. Few are trained in finance and accounting. Many abhor statistics, numbers, and mathematics. The sender has to take special measures to make sure the communication is as simple as possible. Without forethought, the channel can get overloaded and the message will not get through. An example might be helpful.

Several years ago the U.S. Congress passed a bill giving the elderly prescription coverage under Medicare called Medicare Part D. Holding my elderly mother's power of attorney and armed with a Ph.D. in accounting, I thought that selecting the best insurance plan for her would be easy. Was I ever wrong. I'm convinced that the D in Part D stands for dumbfounding because of the staggering number of choices. The government turned the program over to hundreds of private insurers who, generally stated, charged what they wanted to cover the cost of the drugs they wanted to offer.

In my mother's state there were literally 30 different plans offering hundreds of different enrollment options to cover so-called formularies of different patented and/or generic prescription drugs at different prices. To compound the selection problem, enrollees had to sign up for a year-long plan while the insurance companies could change the drugs they would cover on short notice. The amount of literature and materials from the insurance companies was daunting. The number of plans, the complexity of the alternatives, and the legalese of the language was simply paralyzing. At the end of the review process I suffered a case of information overload. I eventually selected a plan hoping, but not knowing, if it was the best one for her. I could have changed my choice a year later but decided against it rather than going through the same process again.

This story is relevant to church financial reporting. Whereas I might be dumbfounded, confused, uncertain, and perhaps angered by my dilemma, a church member faced with the information overload from church financial reports might say, "Why do they have to make these financial statements so difficult to understand?" or "What good are financial statements if no one understands them?" Sound familiar?

Research conducted at a large university in the Northwest studied people's capacities to process financial information. Although the study was limited, it did point out that people are unable simultaneously to process

Example 3.1: Sample Financial Statement

	Balance 12-31-X1	Transfers to Accounts	Income	Disbursements	Balance 11-30-X2
1. HOME OPERATING	($4,477.31)	($173,123.05)	$164,685.82		($12,884.54)
2. Salaries & Wages			134,728.39	$134,728.39	
3. Pension & Health			12,114.12	12,114.12	
4. Janitor Supplies			996.24	996.24	
5. Church Supplies			1,098.00	1,098.00	
6. Office Supplies			3,273.27	270.00	3,543.27
7. Utilities			10,302.96	59.15	10,362.11
8. Conferences & Conventions			2,850.83	333.68	3,184.51
9. Church Publications			1,027.32	41.50	1,068.82
10. Insurance			3,551.10		3,551.10
11. Continuing Education	400.00		400.00		400.00	400.00
12. Youth Ministry			1,015.10	340.00	1,355.15
13. Welfare			407.98	230.00	637.98
14. Scholarships Paid			200.00		200.00
15. Vacation Bible School			228.84	246.97	475.81
16. Community Relations			286.90	30.00	316.90
17. 1% of H-O to Church College			1,271.09		1,271.09
18. **Total Home Operating**			**$166,237.12**	**$175,303.49**	
19. RADIO BROADCAST	488.80		4,240.50	4,118.76	610.54
20. BROADCAST EQUIPMENT	53.68			16.67	37.01
21. SUNDAY SCHOOL	429.17		1,090.50	1,370.75	148.61
22. REPAIRS	3,662.16		4,471.87	6,434.39	1,699.64
23. DEBT & CAP. IMPROVEMENT	2,877.70	(280.00*)	5,101.93	2,500.00	5,199.63
24. SCHOOL BOOKS & SUPPLIES	552.98		6,426.00	5,602.41	1,376.57
25. PERFORMING ARTISTS	72.29				72.29
26. CHOIR MUSIC	90.41			90.41	
27. CHURCH LIBRARY	50.00			27.50	22.50
28. NON-BUDGET ITEMS			1,903.50	1,893.02	10.48
29. HYMNAL FUND	(16.49)		301.40	230.50	54.41
30. VAN FUND	1,289.31	123.86	700.28	485.03	1,627.92
31. OFFICE EQUIPMENT	243.40		2,012.00	2,670.00	(414.60)
32. COMPUTER			3,350.00	2,601.15	748.85
33. MEMORIAL	325.00			262.05	62.95
34. STUDENT TUITION AID	100.00	(472.50)	4,111.98	455.00	3,284.48
35. INSURANCE REPAYMENT			3,940.00	2,372.02	1,567.98
36. SPECIAL SUNDAY			525.50	221.22	304.28
37. **Total Local Accounts**			**$204,412.27**	**$206,654.37**	
District $21,792.62					
38. World Missions			11,267.75	11,267.75	
39. Food Pantry			8,244.00	8,244.00	
40. Radio Show			395.00	395.00	
41. Television Show			820.80	820.80	
42. World Relief			309.00	613.80	(304.28)
43. Good Samaritan Home			186.00	186.00	
44. Agate Memorial			123.00	123.00	
45. Foundation			59.00	59.00	
46. University			7.00	7.00	
47. Bible Translators			24.02	24.02	
48. Deaf Program			4.00	4.00	
49. Bradshaw Memorial			249.05	249.05	
50. Flood Victims Program			20.00	20.00	
51. Armed Forces Program			49.00	49.00	
52. Christmas Offering			35.00		35.00
53. **TOTALS**	**$6,171.10**		**$226,204.89**	**$228,716.27**	

*Interest in forbearance transferred to Home Operating Account 12-3-X2.

Church Treasurer Signature: *Conrad Confusion*

and understand many different financial variables. If, for example, your monthly financial reports lists

(1) five types of cash inflow and total inflows (6 items),
(2) ten types of expenditures and total expenditures (11 items),
(3) the excess of cash inflows over expenditures or vice versa (1 item), and
(4) the beginning and ending cash balances (2 items),

there are already a total of 20 pieces of information. If budgeted information is presented side by side with the actual amounts, the number of pieces of financial data increases to 40. If the statement also includes year-to-date columns, both actual and budgeted, you now have 80 pieces of financial data to comprehend. Even without budgeted data, the situation can get out of hand.

Example 3.1 presents an actual church financial statement given to me by a church treasurer. Some account names have been changed to avoid denominational references. Note the clutter due to an overwhelming number of items, numbers for each line, and reporting in pennies! Just eliminating the number for each line would make the statement appear less formidable. The statement has over 250 pieces of information if you count the data, headings, line numbers, account names, and money amounts. Further, some of the money amounts are negative; these have to be processed in a second step, in reverse of positive amounts. An untrained person cannot digest the information, ask appropriate questions, and make correct decisions based upon this report.

To summarize, faulty communication can be caused by both senders and receivers of messages. What can be done about it? Educating the receivers is not the most efficient alternative. The easiest and most direct avenue is to have church treasurers—the senders—refine their product to allow the receivers to better use the reports. In communicating financial information, your aim is to satisfy the requirements of the users.

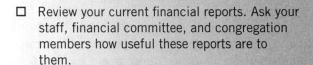

ACTION ITEMS

- ☐ Review your current financial reports. Ask your staff, financial committee, and congregation members how useful these reports are to them.
- ☐ What can you do to provide more relevant, easily-digestible financial information?

3. PRINCIPLES OF FINANCIAL REPORTING

There is no standard set of financial reports that is equally effective for every church. Reports must be tailored to the personalities, circumstances, and educational level of the users in each church. The content, design, and manner of presentation of reports are all important factors in communication.

One church may rely on one technique, and another within the same denomination may use a different method set of reports. Yet, at the end of the day, the effectiveness of planning, controlling, and decision-making depends largely on the ability of the financial reports to help people make correct decisions.

There are five key principles of financial reporting that transcend all organizations. Where applicable, these principles should be used for reports of church financial information, whether for dissemination to the membership or for internal use by church managers. Not all principles apply to every report. A review of these principles should provide you with a wealth of ideas for modification of your own reports. The discussion of each reporting principle is followed by a salient question relating to your church's financial reports which can be answered yes or no. For the following five questions, work on changing any no's to yes. Keep a list of problem areas to address.

RESPONSIBILITY REPORTING

Area reporting

Responsibility reporting is based on the organizational structure of the church. For example, the church might have centers, departments, committees, or programs for worship, missions, buildings and grounds, education, youth, administration, music, kitchen, and so on. The thrust of responsibility accounting is that financial reporting is done by specific area rather than in the aggregate.

Thus, for example, salaries and wages are spread out among the various centers rather than just the grand total being reported as an expense. Also, centers that produce both revenues and costs, such as schools, show a matching of these items. With responsibility reporting, users can better assess the performance of individual centers and, in the process, of their administration.

Question 1: From a quick read of your church's financial reports, can you determine the amount spent on buildings and grounds so far this year and how much is left in the budget for buildings and grounds?

EXCEPTION REPORTING

Highlight exceptions

Financial report users should be directed to the out-of-the-ordinary performance. If performance is generally as expected, then valuable energy and time is not wasted looking at acceptable, expected results. Some treasurers accomplish this by preparing a percentage variance when actual and budgeted data is presented side by side.

For example, if actual weekly offerings are shown as $226,221 and expected offerings were $229,845, the shortfall of 1.6 percent is indicated. Thus, users do not have to calculate the difference of $3,624 and ponder whether that is significant. They are advised that the difference is 1.6 percent of the budget which, by any standard, can be chalked up as a small deviation. But if actual offerings are $188,473 and budgeted offerings were $229,845, the shortfall is 18 percent, which is major and should be written in red or in capitals.

Question 2: From a quick read of your church's financial reports, can you determine which item, program, or activity is doing significantly better than anticipated?

SUMMARIZED REPORTING

Summarize data

The kind of information needed by the membership is not the same as that needed by the finance committee. The finance committee keeps a close eye on all church activities. It needs details, sometimes pages of them. The general members do not keep a close eye on anything. They just want to know if the church can pay its bills. Summarized data is all they need. Hence, one church financial statement cannot serve the needs of all constituents. Different audiences need different reports. Not only are perspectives different but, as discussed earlier, so are capabilities. Using the organization chart from Example 1.1 in the first chapter of this book, the most detailed financial report should be provided to members of the finance committee; less detailed information should be provided to the administrative board; and yet less detail should be provided to the congregation.

Question 3: Does your church prepare several different financial reports for the same time period, each addressed to a different audience?

COMPARATIVE REPORTING

Compare data

Often absolute financial figures mean nothing. A report that says that weekly offerings were $20,000 doesn't impart any real information. To be valuable, data must be compared with something—compared with a budget, with last week's offerings, with last year's offering for the same week, and so on. The reader must be able to grasp quickly how the actual results compare with some yardstick.

Guiding users through the data by showing relationships is important. For example, a deviation from expected offerings might not be brought to the attention of readers properly if the treasurer merely shows weekly offerings in one column and year-to-date offerings in a second column, with no reference to budgeted expectations. Comparative reporting means two amounts are compared meaningfully not that the two columns are simply presented side by side.

Question 4: From a quick read of your church's financial reports, can you determine if vehicle expenses for all activities this year compare unfavorably with those for last year?

INTERPRETIVE REPORTING

Interpret data

Interpretive reporting means adding meaningful comments to money amounts to help readers digest the information. Few church treasurers employ this technique. Instead, many treasurers feel compelled to show up at every meeting where his or her financial report is discussed in order to explain it. But if a few sentences of explanation were added at the bottom, the report might be able to stand alone. Commentary might indicate significant variances from the budget and, when known, the reasons for the variances. Interpretive reporting is especially helpful to those persons unable or unwilling to read financial reports.

Question 5: Have your church's financial reports ever included a written analysis?

OTHER FACTORS IN FINANCIAL REPORTING

The five principles of financial reporting just discussed are basic to a good financial reporting system. In addition, several others factors can assist the reader to understand the message. For the following six questions your answer should be no. Again, note the problem areas to address.

1. Reports should be accurate. Nothing discredits a report more than for a reader to find an inaccuracy, no matter how small. When an error is found, it jeopardizes the credibility of all the other figures on the report, the accounting system that processed data into information, and the treasurer, who failed to find the error. Church financial reports must be proofed before they are distributed. Many public accounting firms proof financial reports three times before they issue them!

Question 1: Has anyone ever found an error in your church's financial reports?

2. Reports should be simple and clear. Cluttered statements like the one in Example 3.1 should be avoided. Information should be arranged so that the reader can secure the essential facts in a reasonable period of time and with a minimum of effort. When necessary, lay terms can be substituted for accounting terms. Similarly, accounts that puzzle readers month after month can be renamed for financial reporting purposes only. After all, if people are continually asking what the quasi-endowment fund is, maybe it would be best to call this line item something else. There is no accounting rule that says that accounts cannot be renamed or grouped creatively for purposes of communication.

Question 2: Has anyone ever noted that your church's financial reports are difficult to understand?

3. Information should be presented meaningfully. Financial data must be displayed in a logical format. The preparer must, in a sense, take the reader by the hand and march him or her through the report. Thus you might show cash inflows as a grouping with an appropriate total before you present cash outflows. Alternatively, with an account like supplies, you might start with a beginning balance, add purchases and subtract amounts used up to derive the ending balance. Logical as this presentation may seem, many users of church financial reports have to grapple with information that is organized in another manner, such as by account number.

Account numbers are necessary to process transactions through the church's accounting system. For instance in the chart of accounts, the pastor's salary expense may be account #500, van expense may be account #510, and so on. However, basing your financial reports on a numbering scheme that was perhaps established decades ago or when the church was started is ludicrous. Even including account numbers in a financial report is a waste of time. Remember the objective of financial reporting is to aid in decision-making not to determine the accuracy of the accounts or list the accounts in the proper order.

Question 3: Are your financial reports in any way based upon your account numbering system?

4. Use whole dollars. Again, the role of financial reporting is to help users plan, control, and make decisions. It is not the role of users to check up on the treasurer's work. Therefore there is little purpose in carrying out amounts to the penny. Whole dollar reporting should be followed.

Round amounts up to the nearest whole dollar if they are more than fifty cents; round down if they are less. If, when arriving at the dollar total, the amount is one dollar different from the correct dollar total, use the correct figure, follow it with an asterisk, and state in a footnote that the $1 difference is due to rounding. If the church treasurer had eliminated pennies in Example 3.1, the report would be ten spaces shorter and appear less complicated. Further, insignificant accounts (i.e. any account with a beginning and ending balance of less than one hundred dollars) can be grouped in one account called, for example, miscellaneous district account. By doing this ten lines would be saved on the statement. Thus it is possible for an account to appear in one month's financial report and not reappear until something significant has again occurred. Few treasurers thin out their reports to make them look less cluttered. Try it; your readers will like it.

Question 4: Do you include cents in the figures you present in your church's financial reports?

5. The cost of report preparation should be considered. All reports have a cost. Whether a preparer gets paid for services or is a volunteer, the church uses resources—human resources—in the preparation of the report. The church should have only those reports prepared where the benefits of preparation exceed the costs of preparation.

Benefits versus costs

Most church leaders agree that the benefits of preparing monthly financial reports and an annual financial report exceed the costs because these provide congregations with the raw materials necessary to plan, control, and make decisions. Put differently, these reports are a natural outgrowth of the accounting process. Likewise, the benefits of complying with the requests by denominational authority and the Internal Revenue Service for specific reports or information are seen as greater than the costs of their preparation.

But the same rationale does not apply to other reports requested by boards, committees, or members. These groups or individuals may not think in terms of costs. They might think that information is free, and all you have to do is look it up. When someone asks you for information that is not readily available, let them know the cost. You will save time, and the church will conserve its resources.

Question 5: In your opinion, does the cost of preparation of any of your church's financial reports exceed the benefits to the church?

6. Reports should be timely. A report is like a fish; the older the information the less useful it is. If reports are to be used for every monthly meeting of the finance committee or administrative board, they should be available for the meeting. For a group to meet without financial information may not only be a waste of their time but may imply that they can proceed without reports. It's a bad precedent. Timeliness of information is another key to useful reports. It serves no purpose to furnish anyone a June 30 financial report in mid-July that includes all transactions up to April 15. A June 30 report should include the result of all activity up to June 30.

When processing lags develop, financial reports, like fish, begin to give off an odor. I've seen programs overspend their annual budgets because spending ran several months ahead of the reports. Think of the dire consequences to the nation's banking system if withdrawals of cash were recorded several months after the funds were withdrawn!

Question 6: Do any of your church's financial reports omit up-to-date, almost real-time, information?

By employing the preceding principles and factors you will help make your financial presentations more useful to users. With each improvement the message will get clearer because the channel of communication will get stronger.

ACTION ITEMS

- [ ] Which of these reports—comparative, summary, or interpretive—do you currently provide to your committees and/or congregation?
- [ ] What are the challenges of creating different reports for different audiences? What are the benefits?
- [ ] What will it cost you—whether in dollars, time, or manpower—to provide alternative reports? In what ways will the benefits outweigh the costs?

4. DIFFERENT AUDIENCES, DIFFERENT REPORTS

Different audiences

As noted earlier, there are several different audiences for church financial statements, each with its own capacity to understand and need for information.

First, there is the general membership. Members use financial statements to help them reach certain conclusions on the status of the church. For example, if the church is doing well financially, members will generally place more confidence in the abilities of the church's leadership. They are more apt to attend church activities, handle jobs for the church, and give for special needs. Further, knowing that the church is financially strong takes pressure off individual members for financial support.

When the opposite financial condition exists, membership confidence and support may be lacking. You might hear a lot of grumbling. Members might be torn between giving money to help the church survive, or withholding their money from the group who has mismanaged it. Uncertainty causes confusion; confusion causes anger. As in sports, people like to be associated with a winner. Thus knowing how the church is doing and whether or not the church can pay its bills are pivotal to the membership.

A second audience is composed of the finance committee, administrative board, program leaders, pastors, and, in large churches, full-time business administrators. These groups need detailed information both to manage current operations and to plan for the future. As a consequence the financial statements provided to these groups should be much more extensive than those provided to the general membership. And if the church retains a certified public accountant to conduct a full-fledged yearly audit, the financial statements will be prepared according to generally accepted accounting principles.

The third audience for church financial statements is composed of banks that have loaned the church funds, trustees who are responsible for the repayment of capital to bondholders (those who hold church bonds issued to finance church expansion or modernization), the Internal Revenue Service, and the church's higher denominational authority. Each of these users will specify the form and content of the financial statements that satisfy its particular needs.

The presence of different audiences means that several different financial reports will have to be prepared to cover the same period. Thus, there is no such thing as "the" financial report. Those church treasurers who attempt to appease all users with a single report have their priorities mixed up. A treasurer's goal should not be to minimize the time spent on preparing reports but to maximize the usefulness of the reports in helping people make appropriate decisions. Just as an automobile manufacturer produces a plethora of different kinds of cars for different markets, effective church treasurers produce several different financial reports for different audiences.

REPORTING TO THE GENERAL MEMBERSHIP

Keep it simple

Members need summary information presented to them in the simplest form possible to enable them to assess the church's financial condition. Spare them the details; spare them the jargon. That means that the monthly, quarterly, and annual reports to members need not be comprehensive or lengthy. A few sentences of narrative interpretation will make the reports more useful to this audience. Your goal is to develop a one-page monthly financial report. Be careful, though; the church treasurer who contributed to Example 3.1 did create a one-page report. But it is confusing. One page, therefore, does not mean a commitment to reduce the font size and completely fill up an 8½ x 11 piece of paper. It means evaluating the needs of your members and the financial activities of the church. It means presenting only the important facts and comparative relationships. It means leaving plenty of white space.

The annual financial report too must be well thought out. A one-page overview of activities and, in a few churches, the traditional list of individual donors, name by name, should suffice. You might add a note that a more detailed presentation of financial affairs has been prepared for the finance committee or administrative board and is available upon request at the church office. Having a few members request copies of a more comprehensive and complex report is far better than overwhelming all members.

Most of the church financial reports intended for the general membership that I have seen do not "pass the test." In fact, many churches seem to share the same dilemma. The problem stems from blindly following the method of presentation used by the previous treasurer. This year's treasurer mimics the predecessor and that one mimics the earlier one, and on and on to the origins of the church. And of course each month that a report was distributed, members would ask, "Why do they have to make these financial statements so difficult to understand?" and "What good is a financial statement if no one understands it?" A variant of this dilemma is to blindly issue the reports provided by the church's computer software. It's easy, but is it understandable?

My suggestion for treasurers who have fallen into these traps is to commit to break from tradition. In other words, you need to design a new, one-page report.

New design

You might find it helpful to find out what other churches are doing, within your denomination and outside of it. Your streamlined, easy-to-understand, one-page report may be the biggest legacy you'll leave to the church and the next treasurer. You might have to experiment for several months using different terminologies, formats, and accounts. Let the congregation know what you are doing. Insert a paragraph in the Sunday church bulletin that notes that you are experimenting with alternative ways of presenting the church's financial information in order to improve its clarity. Point out that you will try several different approaches over the next several months and that all comments are welcome.

One final word about reporting to the membership. It concerns the whereabouts of the cash in the church's cash accounts and investments. Many churches have checking accounts, which may be interest bearing or passbook savings accounts or certificates of deposit with a specific maturity. Some churches also have investments in the form of stocks, bonds, or real estate. In monthly financial reports to the general membership, it is unwise to be specific about the exact location of these assets. It is necessary only to present the

Example 3.2: Sample Cash Balance Statement

Checking account, Eastern National Bank, noninterest bearing		$1,000
Savings accounts		
Southern State Bank, 5½ percent	$2,000	
Northern Trust Bank, 6 percent	1,500	3,500
Six-month certificate of deposit		
Western Hills Bank of Commerce 7 percent, matures 4/15/XX	10,000	$14,500

Example 3.3: One-Page Financial Report

Contributions in April	$ 8,090
Expenditures in April	13,290
Cash deficit for the month	(5,200)
Cash Balance, April 30	15,750
Commitments for May	6,500

The cash balance of $15,750 on April 30th is approximately $6,000 lower than the expected balance at this date. This is due to the unplanned payment of $6,100 made in April to repair the damage caused by the flooded basement in early March. Other contributions and expenditures were as expected.

balances of each category in their broadest terms. For example, to state that the church has cash accounts of $14,500 consisting of $1,000 in a checking account, $3,500 in savings accounts and $10,000 in a certificate of deposit is sufficient. Some churches are much more specific and present something like the following:

Second-guessers

Although this method is informative, mentioning banks, maturity dates, and interest rates can be dangerous. The danger comes from members using the information to second-guess those church leaders responsible for making financial decisions.

For example, there's the question of banks. Given the information above, a member is likely to note that a son of a church member has just been appointed assistant vice president of the Bank of X and recommends that you move some or all of the church's funds to his bank. Yet the recommending member probably knows nothing about the financial condition of the bank, whether it has incurred recent losses and/or whether it is federally insured.

Then there is the maturity of the certificate of deposit. It's easy to be critical of the church's six-month maturity when it is obvious to some that a longer maturity usually commands a higher interest rate. Then again, if the church had a longer maturity, some people would comment that a six-month maturity would have been far superior because interest rates were expected to rise in the near future.

Finally, and most importantly, there is the interest rate debate. Even if the church were earning 16 percent on its funds, some member would point out that he or she knows of a higher-yielding investment for the church. No matter what the church was earning on its funds, some members would indicate that it was unwise for the church not to be earning a higher return. And if the church is not earning any interest at all, such as on its checking account, some member is bound to have a meltdown!

In summary, the second-guessing related to which banks, maturities, and interest rates the church has committed to can destroy overall confidence in the investment decision-makers. Those members making offhand comments typically do not have all the facts and have never had the fiduciary responsibility of managing the church's assets.

Risk versus return

The goal of the church's investment decision-makers, whether treasurer, finance committee, or administrative board, is not to maximize the return on its money. If that were the case, they would make risky investments. The goal of the decision-makers is to protect the church's capital and, in the process, earn some interest. *The key is not to lose money.*

What most second-guessing members fail to realize is that in finance there is a tradeoff between risk and return. That is, those who are willing to take the biggest risks get the greatest return, and those less willing to

Example 3.4: One-page Financial Report

	Beginning Balance 11/30/20XX	Receipts	Disbursements	Ending Balance 12/31/20XX
Checking Account	$20,000	$14,000	$(8,000)	$26,000
Saving Accounts	5,000	1,000		6,000
Total	$25,000	$15,000	$(8,000)	$32,000
General Fund	$12,000	$13,000	$(6,000)	$19,000
Buildings and Grounds	7,000	1,500	(1,800)	6,700
Missions Fund	6,000	500	(200)	6,300
	$25,000	$15,000	$8,000	$32,000
Total Receipts		$15,000		
Total Disbursements		8,000		
Net Increase		$ 7,000		

take risks get a lower return. And, to repeat, the goal is not to lose any of the church's money.

Benchmarking

I trust the investment decision-makers reach their conclusions about the safety of specific banks, the trend in interest rates, and the risks inherent in each investment in a prudent manner. If their wisdom is continually criticized and if they eventually yield to pressure, the church might be headed for trouble. Some churches have suffered large losses in search of a higher rate of return. Can your church handle the risk? If not, don't foster the second-guessing by providing ammunition in the financial report. Keeping the presentation general implies that it's someone else's responsibility to work out the investment details.

Annual reports, however, should be more specific, providing full details and possibly even the average rate of return earned on cash assets in the 12-month period. In churches that elect officers and appoint committees annually, it is useful to know how the outgoing group has managed the funds. This information can provide a benchmark for the incoming group as well as provide information to those who might seek to hold an office or serve on the finance committee.

Several examples of one-page monthly financial reports to the general membership are presented in Examples 3.3 to 3.7. Please review these examples. You are likely to find some ideas to improve your financial reporting.

REPORTING TO MANAGEMENT

Financial reports are also needed by church management–the finance committee, the administrative board, business administrators, program leaders, the pastor, and so on. As noted, financial reports prepared for this group need to be more extensive and detailed than reports provided to the general membership. Pay particular attention to the principles and factors of sound financial reporting presented earlier. Thus heeding the responsibility reporting concept, the chairperson of the Christian education program will receive only the financial details for his or her operation. All other financial data is irrelevant to that program.

Example 3.5: One-Page Financial Report

Revenues	Actual	Budget
Weekly offerings	$10,000	$9,800
Restricted donations	6,000	5,000
School tuition	8,000	8,000
Interest on savings	400	500
Other	500	550
Total revenues	**$24,900**	**$23,850**

Expenditures		
Pastor's salary	$2,000	$2,000
Pastor's allowances	750	800
Office salaries	1,200	1,400
Utilities	400	250
School expenses	8,500	7,800
Mortgage payment	1,000	1,000
Purchase of computer	3,000	3,000
Payout of restricted donations	4,900	4,900
Other	70	600
Total expenditures	**$22,220**	**$21,750**

Excess of revenues over expenditures	$2,680	$2,100
Cash balance, beginning of month	32,000	
Cash balance, end of month	**$34,680**	

Cash composition		
Checking account, petty cash	$3,280	
Savings accounts	6,400	
Certificate of deposit	25,000	
	$34,680*	

* Restricted donations yet to be disbursed total $12,100. Board-designated restrictions of cash total an additional $5,000. The remainder is unrestricted.

Restricted donations		
Beginning balance of restricted gifts		$11,000
Restricted donations received		
For new bus	$5,000	
For new computer programs	1,000	6,000
		$17,000

Restricted donations paid out		
Paid for kitchen equipment	$900	
Paid to world missions	4,000	4,900
Ending balance of restricted gifts		**$12,100**

Example 3.6: One-Page Financial Report

	Actual	Budget
Unrestricted revenues	$12,000	$11,000
Unrestricted disbursements		
Salaries	-3,000	-3,000
Administration	-4,000	-3,500
School expenses	-3,500	-4,000
Excess of unrestricted revenues over unrestricted disbursements	$1,500	$500
Restricted revenues		
Foreign missions	$1,000	$3,000
New van	20,000	20,000
Restricted disbursements		
Purchased new van	-20,000	-20,000
Excess of restricted revenues over restricted disbursements	$1,000	$3,000
Total excess of revenues over disbursements	$2,500	$3,500
Add beginning cash balance	20,000	
Ending cash balance	**22,500**	

Analysis of Ending Cash Balance

Undisbursed, restricted amounts	$7,000
Needed to pay existing bills	5,000
Unrestricted, uncommitted cash	10,500
Ending cash balance	**$22,500**

Author's note: Year-to-date columns could be added to this report if desired.

On the other hand, those responsible for or needing to know about all church activities will receive a more complete financial report. Remember, different audiences mean different reports. Following the principle of exception reporting, direct the attention of users to those areas that vary significantly from expectations, whether good or bad. Further, present data in comparative form, provide summarized data when appropriate to gain a perspective, and, when necessary, include interpretive comments.

As with reports to the general membership, you have to rethink your goals in reporting financial information to managers. If there have been complaints about understandability, new formats should be developed.

A period of experimentation might be necessary before both you and the users settle on a particular format and contents. If no one is asking for information that the reports do not contain, it could be that the reports are too extensive. To use a sports analogy, you might be giving everyone a play-by-play presentation when all they want is the final score.

Various types of managerial financial reports are found among churches, depending on such things as their size, the sophistication of their managers, their use of computers, and whether the church receives an audit by a CPA. For instance, Example 3.8 is a detailed report for church management, which essentially is a more comprehensive version of the one page report to members. It includes details of expenditures from programs and functions that are summarized in the membership presentation. Managers need details to evaluate the various activities of the church.

If the church uses a computer software package for its accounting and finance, the reports to management typically are natural outgrowths of the processing of transactions. The reports themselves do differ in format, content, and presentation depending on the vendor. And just because the reports are computer generated doesn't mean that they should be used. I've seen many computerized reports that differed little from the confusing report in Example 3.1.

If a church undergoes a financial audit with an independent CPA, the financial statements are prepared in accordance with generally accepted accounting principles and include several comparative financial statements. The statements will include 1) a Statement of Financial Position, which contains ending balances of assets and liabilities, 2) Statement of Activities, which summarizes overall contributions and expenditure activity for the period, and 3) a Statement of Cash Flows, which presents how the church received or used cash for the same period. Examples of these three statements are presented as Examples 3.9, 3.10, and 3.11. Chapter 5 will cover the topic of audits in greater detail.

To assist managers in getting the maximum benefit from the financial reports, you may prepare some analysis for their review. For example, since a significant part of the church's total expenditures are for wages and salaries, you might want to calculate this percentage relationship and the others presented in Chapter 2 of this book before any meetings where management would receive the financial reports. By providing useful information to decision-makers, your work will have a direct effect on ministry effectiveness.

REPORTING TO OTHERS

Periodically you will have to prepare financial reports for other users, such as the higher denominational authority, the Internal Revenue Service, or, if funds have been borrowed, perhaps a bank. These users typically are quite specific about the financial information they want and the format they want you to use. Banks, for example, may ask to see financial statements that have been either audited or reviewed by a CPA. Bankers are accustomed to reading financial reports that are prepared in accordance with generally accepted accounting principles and that have been prepared by an independent accounting professional. This requirement may exist for each year that the funds are owed. Examples 3.9 through 3.11 illustrate financial reports prepared by independent CPAs.

The Internal Revenue Service (IRS) provides forms for your reports to them. Thus, for example, if your church is subject to taxation on unrelated business income, you would need to file the appropriate form. The IRS seems to have a form for almost every possible event. The

Example 3.7: One-Page Financial Report

		Unrestricted	Restricted	Total
Beg. balance	June 1, 20XX	$4,000	$2,000	$6,000
Receipts	June - 20XX	3,500	1,000	4,500
Disbursements	June - 20XX	-3,200	-1,500	-4,700
End. Balance	June 1, 20XX	$4,300	$1,500	$5,800

Savings accounts	$5,800
+ Checking account	800
= End. Balance	$5,800

Month of June

	Actual	Budgeted
Total unrestricted receipts	$3,500	$4,000
Program/dept. disbursements		
Fellowship	$750	$500
Stewardship	250	100
Education	500	800
Worship	500	500
Buildings and grounds	100	1,000
Outreach	0	100
Evangelism	100	100
Administration	1,000	1,000
Total disbursements	$3,200	$4,100
Net increase or decrease	$300	($100)
Total restricted receipts	$1,000	$1,000
For computer	$400	$0
For altar flowers	100	0
For church college	500	1,000
Restricted disbursements		
Paid to church college	$1,500	$1,500
Net increase or decrease	($500)	($500)

Author's note: Year-to-date columns could be added to this report if desired.

church's CPA can greatly assist the church in complying with any federal, state, and city income tax regulations.

Denominational requirements

The higher denominational authority often requires churches to submit monthly, quarterly, and/or annual financial reports. Usually the church treasurer is provided with copies or examples of the forms, the accounts to use, and definitions of terms. For example, *plate offerings* might be defined as "loose offerings that are unrestricted or undesignated. These are to include all offerings at Easter, Christmas, and so on, if made for general purposes." Likewise, *pledge payments* might "include all amounts placed in regular pledge offering envelopes even from persons making no pledge, whether monies are intended for general operating purposes or designated by the donor." Note the specificity needed to answer treasurers' questions in advance and to promote the preparation of uniform reports by all churches within the denomination. Such uniformity is necessary for higher church authorities to assess the financial condition of churches within their jurisdiction. Without consistency in data collection and reporting, information from different churches might not be comparable. It could be like trying to compare apples and oranges.

Because each user has specific needs, preparing financial reports for others might take considerable time and might be costly. In an attempt to cut the costs of report preparation, some churches organize their accounting system so that, for instance, the report for the higher denominational office can be prepared quickly. This is satisfactory if the system can then be used to prepare reports that are equally useful to the church managers and to the general membership. Often, however, this is not the case, and the church loses more resources by having members and management make decisions without relevant information. Unless your church is required to use particular account forms and formats internally, I suggest that you not let the reporting needs of others dictate what you do internally.

Reporting the financial results of church operations is the end product of the budgeting and accounting process. It should not be an afterthought that results in a mishmash of poorly organized data. It should be well planned and artfully executed.

■ ACTION ITEMS ■

☐ Do you provide a report to your general membership? If so, in what ways has providing the church's financial information been beneficial?

☐ What details do your financial managers need to see in a report to evaluate ministry financial health?

5. STRUCTURE FOR CHANGE

The preceding material has covered the essentials of church financial reporting. At this point you might be one of a tiny group of people bursting with pride because of the exemplary manner in which your church handles this task. Your church may have long recognized that the true purpose of reporting is to communicate information to allow users to make decisions. And to that end, you issue a one page monthly report for the congregation and more extensive monthly reports for church managers.

Alternatively, the preceding material might have exposed a variety of reporting challenges in your church. You still might be using the reports to "check up on" someone or something, might still be stressing accuracy to the penny and might still be exhibiting a "one size fits all" mentality. Change might come slowly.

The purpose in investing time and money in reading this text is to prepare you to help your church. Realize that the change agent is you, not your pastor, not another member of the congregation. Effective church reporting comes from people who want to be effective. You are in the best position to influence improvement and change. Share your concerns; share your wisdom; share your enthusiasm. Your church will benefit from your efforts.

Example 3.8: Detailed Financial Report to Church Management

Summary Page

	Current Month	Year 20X2 To Date	Year 20X2 Budget
Receipts			
Pledged contributions	$32,818	$210,190	$600,000
Nonpledged gifts	1,209	9,371	15,000
Restricted	2,000	6,431	5,000
Other	2,336	49,824	75,000
Total	**$38,363**	**$275,816**	**$695,000**
Disbursements			
Administration	$5,722	$38,082	$76,475
Property	16,997	118,045	218,600
Local programs	20,041	113,460	229,925
Missions	2,304	11,635	85,000
Total	**$45,004**	**$281,222**	**$610,000**
Analysis of cash			
Checking account balances	$1,987		
Money market account	32,802		
Certificate of deposit	15,000		
Total cash at end of month	**$49,789**		

ADMINISTRATION

Administration and finance

	Current Month	Year 20X2 To Date	Year 20X2 Budget
Secretarial salaries	$3,031	$18,377	$36,800
Stationery and printing	282	2,352	4,500
Supplies and Misc. expenses	136	1,837	2,100
Postage	385	2,022	4,400
Telephone	310	2,443	3,800
Annual pledge campaign			600
	$4,144	**$27,031**	**$52,200**

Miscellaneous

	Current Month	Year 20X2 To Date	Year 20X2 Budget
Payroll taxes	$656	$3,966	$9,075
Kitchen manager	250	1,500	3,000
Kitchen manager auto expenses	75	450	900
Church nursery	597	4,275	8,000
Conference--lay delegates		450	600
	$1,578	**$10,641**	**$21,575**

Contingencies

	Current Month	Year 20X2 To Date	Year 20X2 Budget
General contingencies		$410	$2,700
Total administration	**$5,722**	**$38,082**	**$76,475**

Example 3.8: Detailed Financial Report to Church Management (cont.)

PROPERTY
Church plant

Note to bank	$5,160	$30,960	$61,920
Murray note		2,500	6,250
Atherton note	2,499	17,288	30,000
Security system		270	800
Normal maintenance	617	2,825	4,000
Capital maintenance	2,041	15,104	10,000
Salaries--superintendent	416	2,500	5,000
Auto expenses	55	330	660
Custodial salaries	1,386	8,544	16,640
Maid salary	994	5,813	11,400
Laundry	167	786	1,130
Utilities: electric	2,640	14,683	30,000
gas	65	3,736	6,000
water		717	1,000
Insurance		5,249	14,000
	$16,040	$111,305	$198,800

Parsonages

Wildwood utilities	$135	$928	$2,700
Lockewood utilities	139	972	2,400
Peavey housing and utilities	683	4,100	8,200
Parsonage maintenance		740	6,500
	$957	$6,740	$19,800
Total property	**$16,997**	**$118,045**	**$218,600**

LOCAL PROGRAMS AND MINISTRIES
Ministerial and professional supervision

District superintendent	$610	$3,659	$6,098
Denominational fund	126	754	1,256
Pension fund--A	1,327	7,963	13,271
Pension program--ministers	1,741	7,540	15,070
Staff salaries	8,958	53,675	113,100
Staff travel	1,918	7,789	17,400
Medical Insurance	527	3,762	9,205
Professional education	671	1,515	1,800
	$15,878	$86,657	$177,200

Christian education

Literature and audiovisual	$1,296	$2,730	$4,600
Supplies and equipment		40	900
Leadership education	41	135	600
Children's ministries	368	610	1,400
Youth ministries	94	481	2,150
Young adult ministries		135	250
Adult ministries	55	198	400
Sports ministries		225	400
Library		30	100
	$1,854	$4,584	$10,800

Worship

Organists' salaries	$650	$3,900	$7,800
Music and choral supplies	310	1,145	2,000
Training and conference		260	450
Worship materials	44	744	600
Guest musicians		200	1,200
Cleaning--choir robes			275
Music maintenance		1,315	7,800

Example 3.8: Detailed Financial Report to Church Management (cont.)

Youth choir tour			1,000
Concert series		500	500
Altar guild			100
	$1,004	**$8,064**	**$21,725**
Membership and evangelism			
Literature		$372	$2,000
Radio broadcast	$465	3,534	4,800
Revival			1,000
Special activities	190	789	1,000
Promotion	650	9,261	10,000
Bible study		189	250
	$1,305	**$14,145**	**$19,050**
Stewardship			
Job bank			$200
Wills and estate planning			250
Stewardship education			100
			$550
Council on ministries programs			
Council activities		$10	$600
Total local programs/ministries	**$20,041**	**$113,460**	**$229,925**
MISSION OUTREACH			
Apportionments			
World service			$10,482
Conference fund			8,779
Jurisdictional fund			984
Interdenominational co-op			283
Conference of churches	$221	$442	2,375
Special ministerial	29	58	294
Church colleges		750	4,515
Campus ministries	568	1,636	5,677
Black colleges		650	2,137
Ministerial education		500	4,485
Lodi assembly			1,223
Homes for the elderly			979
Missional priorities			1,234
Progress fund	783	2,316	7,831
District missions	690	2,070	6,900
	$2,291	**$8,422**	**$58,178**
Advance specials			
Commission on missions	$13	$213	$8,422
World specials			6,000
Central America work		400	2,250
Alcohol and drug education		200	200
Mission home			2,000
Seacrest Plaza home		1,100	2,750
Soup kitchen		1,200	2,000
Peters Convalescent Center			2,000
Society of St. Blainc		100	1,200
	$13	**$3,213**	**$26,822**
Total mission outreach	**$2,304**	**$11,635**	**$85,000**
Grand total	**$45,064**	**$281,222**	**$610,000**

Example 3.9: Statements of Financial Position

	December 31	
	2008	**2007**
ASSETS:		
Cash and cash equivalents	$ 1,085,996	$ 733,652
Miscellaneous receivables	15,041	14,525
Prepaid expenses	79,706	61,228
Deposits	8,660	16,800
Fixed Assets, net	20,415	27,250
	$ 1,209,818	**$ 853,455**
LIABILITIES AND NET ASSETS		
Liabilities:		
Accounts payable and accrued expenses	$ 65,655	$ 71,461
Net assets:		
Unrestricted:		
Undesignated	1,110,043	716,568
Net investments in fixed assets	20,415	27,250
	1,130,458	743,818
Temporarily restricted	13,705	38,176
	1,144,163	781,994
	$ 1,209,818	**$ 853,455**

Example 3.10: Statements of Activities

	Year Ended December 31					
	2008			2007		
	Unrestricted	Temporarily Restricted	Total	Unrestricted	Temporarily Restricted	Total
SUPPORT AND REVENUE:						
Contributions:						
Weekly contributions	$3,863,540	$ -	$3,863,540	$ 3,951,889	$ -	$3,951,889
Missions contributions	428,017	13,705	441,722	337,004	38,176	375,180
Charity and relief contributions	162,913	-	162,913	200,371	-	200,371
	4,454,470	13,705	4,468,175	4,489,264	38,176	4,527,440
Revenues:						
Special events revenue	221,096	-	221,096	335,105	-	335,105
Merchandise sales	1,517	-	1,517	9,547	-	9,547
Other revenue	75,792	-	75,792	35,860	-	35,860
	298,405	-	298,405	4,869,776	38,176	4,907,952
Total support and revenue	4,752,875	13,705	4,766,580	4,869,776	38,176	4,907,952
RECLASSIFICATIONS:						
Net assets released from restriction upon satisfaction of purpose	38,176	(38,176)	-	19,867	(19,867)	-
EXPENSES:						
Program services:						
Ministry	3,430,879	-	3,430,879	3,808,298	-	3,808,298
Missions	462,580	-	462,580	361,241	-	361,241
	3,893,459	-	3,893,459	4,169,539	-	4,169,539
Supporting activities — general and Administrative	510,952	-	510,952	539,271	-	539,271
Total expenses	4,404,411	-	4,404,411	4,708,810	-	4,708,810
Change in net assets	386,640	(24,471)	362,169	180,833	18,309	199,142
Net assets, beginning of year	743,818	38,176	781,994	562,985	19,867	582,852
Net assets, end of year	$1,130,458	$13,705	$1,144,163	$743,818	$38,176	$781,994

Example 3.11: Statements of Cash Flows

	Year Ended December 31	
	2008	2007
CASH FLOWS FROM OPERATING ACTIVITIES		
Change in net assets	$362,169	$199,142
Adjustments to reconcile change in net assets to net cash provided (used) by operating activities:		
Depreciation	15,484	19,671
Change in:		
Miscellaneous receivables	(516)	3,799
Prepaid expenses	(18,478)	25,030
Deposits	8,140	(100)
Accounts payable and accrued expenses	(5,806)	(21,802)
Missions grant payable	-	(323,000)
NET CASH PROVIDED (USED) BY OPERATING ACTIVITIES	360,993	(97,260)
CASH FLOWS FROM INVESTING ACTIVITIES:		
Acquisition of fixed assets	(8,649)	(20,578)
NET CASH USED BY INVESTING ACTIVITIES	(8,649)	(20,578)
Net change in cash and cash equivalents	352,344	(117,838)
Cash and equivalents, beginning of year	733,652	851,490
Cash and cash equivalents, end of year	$1,085,996	$733,652

Chapter 4

Internal Financial Controls to Minimize the Risk of Embezzlement

by Richard J. Vargo

1. INTERNAL CONTROL OF ASSETS

The protection of assets (cash, equipment, securities, valuables, and so on) is a basic financial management requirement for all organizations, whether large or small, profit-seeking or nonprofit. Unfortunately in most churches the internal control of assets traditionally has been weak. As a consequence about 15 percent of all churches have been, are being, or will be victimized by an unscrupulous employee or member. All denominations and churches, regardless of size, are susceptible to embezzlement.

Dishonest Acts

Embezzlement most frequently occurs because of people pocketing cash. This is not surprising because churches receive and disburse significant amounts of cash, and all too often money is handled in a casual way. Investment securities, jewels, and other valuables, supplies, and equipment have also disappeared from church premises. Few of these cases appear in the newspaper. In fact, in many cases the problems are handled by the leaders of the church, and the employees and congregation never learn of the situation.

Honest Errors

Honest errors also account for significant financial losses. Many church accountants have inherited a set of accounting records that contain errors and cannot be balanced. Errors may have been made years ago, which preclude the current preparation of accurate financial reports. Such situations cause frustration for both the preparers and users of financial information. Although you cannot design a perfect system that detects and prevents all errors, various features can be built into the accounting system to minimize the probability of errors.

Discussing internal controls is never a popular topic. Most of us like to think of our leaders, fellow workers, or members of the congregation as being competent and, above all, honest. Churches that have never experienced the loss and embarrassment that comes with discovering money is missing from the Sunday offering, or bank balances aren't reconciling properly, often fail to see the critical need to have solid internal controls in place. Nonetheless, consider this: your members contribute hard-earned resources to enable the church to spread the word of God—resources that could be used to feed and clothe their own families. Church leaders have a special fiduciary obligation to make sure that all church assets are protected and used properly.

> **Church leaders have a special fiduciary obligation to make sure that all church assets are protected and used properly.**

■ ACTION ITEMS ■

- ☐ Has your church ever had an incident of theft from the offerings or of its other assets?
- ☐ What is the attitude among church leaders regarding implementing sound internal control practices?
- ☐ Based on your church's current internal control practices, how vulnerable do you feel your church is to the threat of embezzlement?

2. GENERAL OBJECTIVES OF INTERNAL FINANCIAL CONTROL

Generally stated, internal financial control can be defined as the various practices adopted by an organization to safeguard assets, check the reliability and procedural accuracy of financial records, and ensure compliance with managerial policies.

Safeguarding assets

In most churches the primary objective of the internal control system boils down to safeguarding the church's assets. In simplest terms this means that the church must establish controls for handling cash receipts and disbursements and all of its other assets. Internal financial controls for cash guard against the understatement of cash receipts and the overstatement of cash disbursements. Internal controls for other assets deal with physical controls, accurate recording, and periodic verification.

Reliability

The need for the internal control system to help produce reliable financial records should not be overlooked. First, accurate recording of all transactions is essential for building trust among those involved in the accounting process and with users of financial reports. A treasurer or finance committee members will grow resentful if he or she receives reports from the bookkeeper that contain entries made to incorrect accounts, or incomplete income and expenditure entries. Church members grow frustrated when their contributions are incorrectly reported, or progress toward meeting pledges is erroneously calculated. After all, members' records of contributions may be used for income tax purposes. Members do not like to call the church office about errors, and the church secretary would prefer not to receive these calls. Rectifying such problems takes time, which is a waste of resources and reflects adversely on the church's financial administration.

Second, users of financial information need reliable reports in order to plan effectively. For instance, finance committee decisions to add a wing, put on a new roof, pave the parking lot, purchase another vehicle, grant a raise, purchase a new organ, re-carpet the hall, or invest excess funds in a certificate of deposit are made based upon the reliability of the information contained in the financial reports. Sound decisions are difficult to make if the financial reports cannot be relied upon! Church managers need reliable data to judge the efficiency of current operations against past or expected performance.

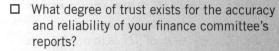

■ ACTION ITEMS ■

☐ What degree of trust exists for the accuracy and reliability of your finance committee's reports?

☐ What decisions are you facing now regarding allocating church funds that necessitate accurate financial information?

☐ To this point, how much time have you had to spend rectifying errors made with church finances or reports?

3. INTERNAL CONTROL PROBLEMS IN CHURCHES

CAUSES AND SOME SUGGESTIONS

Churches encounter cases of misappropriated funds and unreliable financial records as the result of several problems, including 1) the handling of incompatible duties by personnel, 2) the lack of a clear organizational structure, 3) the absence of qualified personnel, 4) the lack of an accounting procedures manual, and 5) the absence of accounting oversight.

These problems exist most commonly in small churches.. Contrary to popular belief, smaller churches have more internal control problems than larger ones. One reason for this: people working in a church have an unstated expectation of trust. We tend to let our guard down and fail to exercise "best practices" when we believe people will do the right thing.

We need to overcome this mindset. The reality is the more attention churches give to implementing and periodically reviewing their internal controls, the fewer problems that are likely to occur.

SEPARATION OF DUTIES

Many functions (duties) performed within a church pertain to financial activities. The church must provide for an adequate separation of duties in order to ensure the accuracy of financial information and to protect the assets. Incompatible duties or functions must be divided; that is they must be performed by different people.

Three basic types of financial activities are performed within a church:

- Authorization of transactions
- Recording of transactions
- Custody of assets

Separate duties

Someone must first authorize a transaction, such as payment for supplies or the receipt of a special gift. Later the transaction must be recorded in "the books." In addition, because many transactions will either immediately or eventually affect an asset, the church must maintain custody of its assets. For an adequate separation of duties to occur, authorization of transactions, recording of transactions, and asset custody should be performed by *different individuals*. When different people handle separate aspects of the same transaction, the likelihood that an error will go all the way through the system is diminished. Each person will, in effect, be checking on the others' work.

In addition to detecting errors, choosing different individuals to authorize, record, and oversee church assets makes it much more difficult for embezzlement to occur. Consider a situation like this: Jennifer, a church bookkeeper, has the authority both to receive cash from members who stop by the church office, and to record cash transactions. Suppose that Lillian, a member of the church, arrives at the office with a $100 special donation. If the transaction is handled properly, Jennifer would place the $100 in a cash box and, later in the day, deposit it in the bank. Further, she would enter the transaction in the accounting records by increasing the cash account and the member's record of contributions by $100.

When duties are not separated, the following could occur: Rather than placing the $100 in the cash box, Jennifer could simply steal the cash. Obviously the cash received could not be recorded because the increase in the cash account would not be matched by an increase in the cash box. But Jennifer would still have to update the accounting records to reflect Lillian's contribution, as Lillian could become suspicious if the payment were not acknowledged. Jennifer could have several ways of accomplishing this, depending on the amount of review given her work. She could merely add the $100 amount to Lillian's contribution record without fear of being found out. And if this action could be detected by someone reconciling total contributions for the year against individual contribution records, Jennifer might, for example, subtract $100 from the contribution record of a member who had moved to a distant state or a member who had recently died.

> **The principle of separating duties to establish internal financial control is violated in the majority of churches.**

Incompatible duties

This example illustrates the point that incompatible duties must be separated for adequate accounting control. This scheme would have been more difficult for Jennifer to undertake if she had access to either the cash *or* the accounting records rather than both.

The principle of separating duties to establish internal financial control is violated in the majority of churches. It could be the single most important cause of misappropriated assets and unreliable financial records. I routinely encounter church financial secretaries and treasurers who "do it all." They claim that they authorize transactions, record transactions, receive cash, and disburse cash. These are incompatible duties and need to be separated. More people need to be involved in the accounting process if the church wants a good internal control system.

Although the best situation is to have different people handle transaction authorization, transaction recording, and asset custody, many churches do not have sufficient personnel to do this. At the minimum, however, all churches should separate the functions of transaction recording and asset custody. For most churches, then, the bookkeeper, or financial secretary, for example, would be responsible only for bookkeeping and accounting. It is important that these individuals not be responsible for counting the weekly offerings, receiving cash from members who come to the office, or paying the bills. Bookkeepers would instead record the details of 1) cash that has been received, counted, and deposited by the counting committee; 2) office cash received, counted, and deposited by another office employee; and 3) disbursements made by authorized persons.

ESTABLISHMENT OF A CLEAR ORGANIZATIONAL STRUCTURE

Corporations typically operate with a clearly defined organizational structure. From the top-down, it is clear who reports to whom and what each position within the company entails. Structure like this helps businesses run more efficiently and effectively.

In many churches people are hired or asked to volunteer a certain number of hours a week to "help out." Quite often church managers do not specify job responsibilities and the order in which each of these responsibilities should be carried out. Many people report to the church each day or week without really knowing what their exact duties are. Some are put to work in accounting and financial reporting without being familiar with established operating procedures. Errors are made, omissions occur, and reports are misdirected because the organizational structure of the church is not well defined. Such fuzziness often leads to internal control breakdowns. Precise job descriptions are just as important to churches as they are to large profit-seeking businesses. In fact, churches need these descriptions even more acutely because, as a non-profit entity, they do not have the readily identifiable "bottom-line" objective of business. Also, many churches use volunteers, who need both supervision and structure to be most effective.

RECRUITMENT OF QUALIFIED PERSONNEL

A church may limit access to assets, separate incompatible duties, and install a host of sophisticated accountability procedures. Yet all of these elements of internal control will be wasted unless one other essential element is present: qualified personnel. Any system is certain to break down if operated by an untrained novice.

What would you think about a church that allowed someone who had never maintained accounting records to keep the books? How about a church that allowed a member whose hobby was computers to design its new computerized accounting system? Or how about a church that requested its bookkeepers, barely out of high school, to design a new financial report for the membership? I trust that you would shake your head in dismay at all three instances. Yet these types of incidents frequently occur.

Continuing education

For a variety of reasons many of us who serve the church in nonministerial positions came without the skills and expertise that we are now developing. If you hold a paid position, you were probably hired for your availability, personality, and reasonable wage requirements. Or you may be a volunteer. During the learning process you have made your share of mistakes. Church officials must recognize that many people working in the church's financial area are novices lacking specific skills.

Church leaders need to commit themselves to a program of continuing education for those involved with finance and accounting, just as businesses do. Church leaders need to get beyond the question of "What does it cost?" and instead ask, "Do the benefits of having qualified personnel outweigh the costs?" Until then, many churches will have a succession of perhaps enthusiastic but under-qualified people handling accounting functions—and will face the accompanying problems of internal control.

Professional training and continuing education in church financial management is available through membership and participation in several organizations, both intradenominational and interdenominational. Your Church Resources (Christianity Today International), the publisher of this book, provides comprehensive resources dealing with church legal, tax, and administrative issues. The National Association of Church Business Administration sponsors a certification program in church business administration (FCBA). Local chapters hold meetings to further the knowledge of church staff members. More information on this organization and other church financial management resources can be obtained online.

ACCOUNTING PROCEDURES MANUAL

Few churches have manuals that specify the manner in which every accounting and financial reporting function is to be handled. Usually the outgoing treasurer or bookkeeper simply meets with the incoming person to discuss these procedures. And sometimes new treasurers and financial secretaries don't receive any instructions at all! They are on their own from the start.

When exiting treasurers and bookkeepers do provide instructions to their successors, the instructions may have limited value for the following reasons:

- Many of the instructions are given orally; newcomers quickly forget them.
- Some of the accounting procedures and methods used by the exiting people are not conveyed to newcomers because of oversights or the haste with which many of these meetings are conducted. Transition in a church is often only given an hour when in fact it may require much more time than this.
- Never having seen the accounting records, many new treasurers and bookkeepers are not in a position to digest all of the instructions quickly. Some have told me that they pretended to understand the instructions so they wouldn't look stupid.

Given the poor instruction provided to many new treasurers and bookkeepers, you cannot expect continuity of internal control procedures from year to year. In fact, in some cases elaborate procedures are established and used effectively one year and totally disregarded the next year. Obviously, it is important that sound internal financial control procedures be developed, installed, and maintained *year after year*.

Church financial leaders need to prepare an accounting procedures manual to guide every step of their accounting and financial reporting process. A manual provides the glue between the old and the new and allows the church to maintain high standards of internal control. Some church groups have prepared treasurer's manuals for their churches. Most of these manuals are useful but tend to emphasize the processing aspects of accounting (which accounts to use) and financial reporting (who receives which report and when). Internal control procedures are often treated lightly, if at all. If a suitable manual is not available, church financial leaders need to design their own manual. The manual should specify the procedures used in:

A. Preparing the budget

B. Handling transactions
Internal Controls
(1) All of the internal controls used when receiving cash or other assets, whether in the offering, at the office, or electronically.
(2) All of the internal controls used when disbursing cash, whether by check, through the petty cash fund, or electronically.

Processing of Transactions
(1) The forms and procedures used to record both cash receipts, including memorials or restricted gifts, and cash disbursements.
(2) The forms and procedures used to record gifts of property and securities.
(3) The accounts used to record the transactions, together with a written description of the types of transactions that should be entered in each account.

C. Assuring reliable recordkeeping
Internal Controls
(1) The procedures used to reconcile totals of cash receipts and cash disbursements against individual amounts.
(2) The procedures used to reconcile church cash records against bank records.

D. Preparing and distributing financial reports
Financial Reporting
  (1) Membership
  (2) Management (finance committees, program leaders, pastor, business administrator, and so on.)
  (3) Others (regional/national church offices, the bank, the Internal Revenue Service, and so on.)

ABSENCE OF MONITORING

In many churches no one has ever monitored the performance of any treasurer or bookkeeper. Such a review might be viewed as unnecessary and, indeed, an affront to the people in those positions.

Although auditing your own staff and volunteers might threaten their egos, not monitoring their work can lead to sloppy records and misappropriated assets. On top of that, just as sexual predators volunteer in churches precisely because they often fail to implement basic screening and selection practices to ward off dangerous individuals, a crooked accountant would be attracted to a situation where work is never checked.

Statistics show that people who misappropriate assets are very often "faithful" employees who perhaps have never even taken vacations, who have perpetrated their schemes over many years, and, interestingly, who have never felt guilty. Some believed that the money they had taken was a pittance compared with their value to the church. In other words, they believed themselves underpaid and under-recognized.

To provide some measure of monitoring, some churches have organized internal audit committees. These committees, often composed of former church treasurers and businesspeople and accountants from the congregation, determine whether the church's procedures and controls are functioning as originally intended. They serve to safeguard assets and to check the accuracy of the accounting information. If nothing else, the mere existence of a committee like this is a psychological deterrent to a person considering embezzlement.

Church leaders sometimes turn to outside help by a certified public accountant once a year—or perhaps every three years—for an internal church financial audit. This topic is covered in detail in chapter five. Generally speaking, a church financial audit involves the investigation and examination of the transactions that underlie the church's financial reports and results in an opinion of those reports. In this process the auditor follows established auditing standards. A thorough review of the internal control system is included. Any defects in the internal control system are brought to the attention of church officials. Charters of some churches specify that annual audits be performed.

THE ARENA OF TRUST

Vulnerability
Most churchgoers want to believe that anyone connected with their church is trustworthy. I frequently hear such comments as, "Who would steal from the house of the Lord?" "If I can't trust people at church, can I trust anyone, anywhere?" And "If someone takes money from the church, he or she probably really needs it."

In other words, people working within a church, whether employees or volunteers, generally think of their environment as being different from other organizations, where people might act dishonestly. For many people, this entire chapter will be disturbing simply because of this belief. In such an arena of trust, people let their guard down. They are less apt to call for strictly enforced internal control procedures. They are also less likely to monitor performance and, if necessary, to take corrective action. Partially as a consequence of this trusting attitude, churches are vulnerable to embezzlement.

Further, many churches hold on to the belief that a church is a ministry and should not be run like a business. This mindset can make churches susceptible to financial misconduct because proper safeguards are not put in place to prevent embezzlement. Selling the necessity of internal control in cases where members are wearing rose-colored glasses or are opposed to internal controls is difficult, to be sure. But internal controls protect church employees, volunteers, and others from needless and damaging accusations or suspicions of embezzlement.

ACTION ITEMS

- [ ] In your church's current configuration, who performs which financial duties?
- [ ] Are their any tasks that require a separation of duties to better safeguard the church's assets as well as the people handling them?
- [ ] Do you have an Accounting Procedures Manual for your church? If not, begin to create one now.
- [ ] Does your church have an internal audit committee? If not, what will you do to create one?

4. INTERNAL CONTROL SYSTEMS

Church financial leaders can tailor internal control practices and procedures to meet their church's specific needs. Each church, regardless of its size, should establish a system of internal control. Implementation of these practices and procedures can substantially reduce but not eliminate the opportunity for misappropriation of assets and the generation of sloppy, unreliable reports. But no system is foolproof. Further, care must be taken in the design of specific controls.

> **Each church, regardless of its size, should establish a system of internal control.**

Be reasonable

For example, a treasurer could mandate that members personally take their weekly offerings to the bank as a way of reducing the risk of embezzlement, require five signatures on all checks to reduce unauthorized cash disbursements, and have all employees fingerprinted and photographed just for good measure. Obviously such practices would be oppressive. Controls should be selected for which the benefits outweigh the cost, both financially and emotionally.

Checklist of benefits

It might be difficult to place a value on sound internal controls. But consider whether it is a benefit to the church to:

- [ ] Remove the temptation to embezzle
- [ ] Prevent a cloud of suspicion from developing over the heads of honest staff members
- [ ] Improve the probability that errors, intentional and unintentional, are discovered
- [ ] Reduce the chance of having to confront a member or employee who has taken funds
- [ ] Reduce the chance of dividing the congregation (or leadership) into those who want to forget a misuse of funds and those who want to take criminal action
- [ ] Reduce the chance of ever having to tell the congregation that some of their contributions have been lost
- [ ] Reduce the chance that you and other church leaders will have to feel embarrassed for allowing an incident to occur
- [ ] Reduce the risk of negative media coverage and the humiliating public portrayal of your church

ACTION ITEMS

- [ ] Which of the benefits listed above gives you new insight into the need for internal controls?
- [ ] In what ways could your financial committee be vulnerable to false accusations of embezzlement or financial mismanagement?
- [ ] What internal controls will you implement to protect your staff and volunteers from false accusations?

5. 50 INTERNAL CONTROL PRACTICES FOR EVERY CHURCH: A TEST

Following are 50 internal controls that should be used by every church. The list is not exhaustive; other practices may be suitable in individual circumstances. For example, larger churches need to employ those controls appropriate for comparably sized commercial enterprises. Many of the sample forms included in this chapter can be re-created electronically with your computer's software. Further, the practices mentioned may not be of equal importance to every church. Some may be very important to your church, and others may be of only secondary importance. I have, however, attempted to make each control relevant to every church.

Additionally, I made no effort to weigh the importance of the different controls. Collectively they are all important because they compose a comprehensive system of internal controls. Almost all of these internal controls can be established and maintained without significant cost to the church.

The 50 controls are presented in the form of a test of your church's current system of internal control. Each practice is introduced, its importance is discussed, and possible violations of the control are indicated. After you read about each control, indicate in the box whether your church presently adheres to this practice.

Answer 'yes' if your church follows the internal control practice in all cases. Answer 'no' if your church does not follow the practice or does not follow the practice consistently. Space for your notes is provided. Be honest with your answers; your church has a lot to gain from this self-test.

Keep in mind that it takes only one 'no' response to show vulnerability. But because the list is not exhaustive (there are probably a thousand-plus controls we could examine), 50 'yes' responses do not mean complete, 100 percent protection. The 50 controls that follow are the most reasonable for all churches, large and small, to use to reduce the risk of embezzlement and the generation of unreliable financial reports.

INTERNAL CONTROLS: GENERAL

The first set of internal controls is general in nature and relates to organizational structure and the overall protection of church assets.

1. Are facilities locked when not in use?

☐ Yes Notes _____

☐ No _____

Analysis
Secure facilities
Securing the premises to safeguard the church's assets is just good common sense. Yet just as we read about people who go on two-week vacations and don't lock their houses, there are some churches that are not adequately secured when not in use. Exterior and interior doors may be unlocked, and windows may be left open. Make sure you have a clear policy on who can have keys to your facility and enforce this policy consistently.

2. Does the church have a written, up-to-date accounting procedures manual?

☐ Yes Notes _____

☐ No _____

Analysis
Accounting procedures manual
The need for an accounting procedures manual to establish accounting procedures, place responsibility,

and assure continuity was discussed earlier. If your church does not currently have such a manual, studies have shown that you're not alone. Of all of the internal controls in this book, this is the control most commonly violated.

3. Are the accounting records and the underlying internal controls audited annually?

☐ Yes Notes _____
_____

☐ No   _____
_____

Analysis
Annual audit
An annual audit offers the church several advantages. First, the fact that everyone knows an annual inspection will occur serves as a deterrent to embezzlement. Second, the auditor has an annual opportunity to evaluate compliance with those internal controls that have been established and to suggest new ways of protecting church assets. Third, in those churches that have a new treasurer every year, the church will be certain to have each treasurer's work reviewed. Thus the auditor can identify and correct any deficiencies before they become standard operating procedures. Fourth, a written policy of annual audits precludes any treasurer from feeling paranoid about members not trusting him or her. Church leaders in those churches having only occasional audits are apt to hear this concern from treasurers in office when an audit is suggested.

Depending on church circumstances, audits are usually performed by a CPA, or an auditor provided by the denominational office.

4. Are the bookkeeper's or treasurer's activities limited to keeping the records of cash collections and preparing the support for disbursements?

☐ Yes Notes _____
_____

☐ No   _____
_____

Analysis
Separation of duties
The need for adequate separation of incompatible accounting duties has already been discussed. To reiterate, the separation of duties is the keystone of a church's internal control system. Keeping the recordkeeping function distinct from the cash handling (asset custody) function will go a long way in reducing the church's risk of embezzlement.

To illustrate, in one church the financial secretary had the responsibility of depositing Sunday offerings in the bank on Monday. The money was counted on Sunday. On Monday, the financial secretary would change the figure on the deposit slip to a lesser amount and keep some money. Because the financial secretary also handled the bookkeeping, the lower amount was recorded on the books. Thus the discrepancy was covered up. Making sure that the financial secretary never had custody of cash would have prevented this.

In another case, a long-time, trusted treasurer, who was the sole signer on checks, decided to steal the church's funds. He accomplished the theft by writing checks to himself and entering the disbursements as payments for supplies. The scheme went on for years. If the treasurer had not had access to both the books and cash, this incident could have been avoided.

5. Does your church's insurance policy include coverage for financial misconduct?

☐ Yes Notes _____
_____

☐ No   _____
_____

Analysis
Insurance coverage
In the past, churches relied on fidelity bonds to provide protection for the church if there was any lapse in the integrity of the accounting system. Today, many churches receive similar coverage through property insurance policies, or this type of policy is purchased in addition to property insurance.

With proper insurance coverage, churches simply can call their agent if they suspect financial wrongdoing, and the insurance company would send auditors to handle the situation in such a way that would prevent legal liability.

6. *Do you utilize an internal audit committee?*

☐ Yes   Notes _____

_____

☐ No   _____

_____

Analysis
Internal audit committee

As previously mentioned, an internal audit committee is usually made up of members with accounting or business backgrounds. They should be familiar with how organizational activities are reflected in the financial statements. They perform some tests of the accounting records. Their tests should be done on a periodic basis (possibly quarterly and annually), but tests done on a sporadic, surprise basis may also be beneficial. If possible, the church's CPA should specify which tests to perform and which procedures to follow.

Internal audit committees—two views

There are two schools of thought on the extensive use of an internal audit committee. One group claims that audits done by nonqualified members are worse than no audits at all. These people assert that the work done by the committee creates a false sense of security for both the accounting staff and the congregation. The other group, of which I am a member, holds that any review is better than no review. People perpetrating dishonest acts do not want their work reviewed by anyone. Having someone examine the records is troublesome to these people—they might get caught! Thus a working internal audit committee is both a psychological and an actual deterrent. A word of caution: an internal audit committee does not replace the need for professional audits by an independent CPA.

7. *Are new accounting personnel screened?*

☐ Yes   Notes _____

_____

☐ No   _____

_____

Analysis
Repeat offenders

Amazingly enough, 70 percent of all embezzlers are repeat offenders. This alarming statistic is relevant to churches for several reasons. First, few dishonest church accountants are ever prosecuted. As noted earlier, the matter is often hushed within the church. Unfortunately, this sometimes means that the perpetrator is free to repeat the scheme in other churches. And that has occurred.

In one case, a treasurer embezzled cash from Sunday offerings that he counted himself. After he was caught, church leaders told him he was never to set foot in the church again. Not two years later he surfaced as the treasurer of a similarly sized church of the same denomination 20 miles away! No one from the new church bothered to inquire about the treasurer's past. Similar cases have involved salaried bookkeepers who embezzled a succession of churches over a long (and probably prosperous) career.

Screening prospective (and probably underpaid) employees and volunteers is not a pleasant task. In many cases congregations are so happy to receive the services that they never make background checks of the individuals. Additionally, screening people to work in the church may seem distasteful. (Remember our previous discussion on the arena of trust earlier in this chapter.) It is, nonetheless, a prudent task. Resources, such as *Screening & Selecting Church Workers* (Your Church Resources/Christianity Today International), are available to assist you.

8. **Has the church prepared an organizational chart for the accounting/financial area which is followed consistently?**

    ☐ Yes Notes _____
    _____

    ☐ No   _____
    _____

Analysis

Organizational chart
It is important that the church have an organizational chart that specifies the position responsible for each accounting function. Of equal importance, the organizational chart needs to be followed. Many churches have a written organizational structure, but the structure is violated almost every week.

For instance, in some churches ushers who collect the weekly offering are people who are tardy for the start of the service and who sit in the last pew. Ten minutes before the offering is collected, they are recruited in an equally haphazard fashion, even though a counting committee has officially been given the task. Specific functions must be handled by the individual or groups assigned to them.

Pastor's involvement
Another aspect of this control involves the relationship between the accounting/finance area and the religious leader of the church. In many churches pastors become heavily involved with financial administration even though they are not given that responsibility on the organizational chart. They become involved for several reasons.

First, the pastor is likely to spend more hours at the church than anyone else and therefore be available to make many financial decisions. Second, the pastor is the religious leader of the church and is typically well respected by the congregation. His or her opinion is often solicited, and people comply with his or her requests. But typically the pastor is not trained in accounting or financial management and thus not truly able to serve as the final authority in these matters.

For example, a pastor might tell the church treasurer that he or she had used a counter check at the bank to withdraw some of the church's funds for a particular purpose. Some treasurers would overlook the pastor's withdrawal of funds in this manner, even though the church's disbursement procedures were probably violated.

Third, pastors naturally desire information about the financial viability of their churches. This need can inadvertently lead to an increasing involvement. One pastor in central California was so involved in financial affairs that he managed to sell the church building!

Therefore, some churches prohibit their pastors from counting money, signing checks and keeping financial records. I am not suggesting keeping pastors from the financial information necessary to operate their churches. Information should be freely transmitted as necessary. But internal control is best maintained when those given responsibilities by the organizational chart carry out their duties precisely as planned.

9. **Are the accounting records safeguarded at all times?**

    ☐ Yes Notes _____
    _____

    ☐ No   _____
    _____

Analysis

Safeguard records
Special control should be exercised over the accounting records and financial data. All of the records and underlying source documents, such as invoices and payroll data, should be kept at the church. Electronic documents and records should be secured by restricting access to specific individuals and maintaining close controls over computer access. Be sure to change computer passwords frequently, update virus protection regularly, and perform backups with an external hard-drive, flash drive, or even through an off-site backup service, which can provide disaster recovery services as well.

Paper documents should be safeguarded by making sure that files are 1) not destroyed, altered, or tampered with during office hours, and 2) properly secured when the office is closed.

In smaller congregations the problem is more acute because many treasurer perform tasks at home. Church records and/or laptop computers have been stolen from the backseats of treasurers' automobiles or lost by treasurers. Any time accounting records are moved from location to location there is added risk of loss. For treasurers working at both the church office and at home, be sure dual protection is in place to safeguard hard copy and electronic records and reports. It's very easy, simple, and affordable now for treasurers to have access to the church's computer system from home through services such as PC Anywhere® or an online accounting package, such as Quickbooks®. By utilizing remote access through these services, church financial leaders reduce the risk of compromising the confidentiality of certain records, plus records are less likely to be lost or stolen.

INTERNAL CONTROLS: CASH RECEIPTS

The next set of internal controls concerns the handling of the church's cash receipts.

10. Are members encouraged to give electronically, or to use offering envelopes?

☐ Yes   Notes _____

☐ No   _____

Analysis
Electronic giving versus envelopes
Many churches collect weekly offerings and contributions electronically. From an internal control standpoint, electronic giving provides one of the safest ways for a church to receive and record contributions. Plus, online giving promotes consistent giving, whether or not the churchgoer is in attendance at weekend services. Electronic giving helps with cash flow.

The more automated the collection process is, the more efficient and safer it is.

For churches that have not yet incorporated e-giving into their financial practices, envelopes continue to serve a dual purpose: 1) they protect members' offerings until they can be counted, and 2) they provide the basis for recording the contribution in the church's accounting records. For churches that continue to favor this method of receiving contributions, the envelopes should be retained by the treasurer, similar to the handling of monthly bills, invoices, and other business documents. The envelopes are essential if total or individual contributions need to be verified by or for the church members. Such verification may be necessary for members having to support their figures on their federal and state income tax returns.

Recent tax laws have changed the rules for substantiating charitable contributions. Now, giving envelopes are no long valid for verifying your offerings.

11. Are collection plates or baskets numbered so you can verify that you have received all offerings?

☐ Yes   Notes _____

☐ No   _____

Analysis
Numbered offering plates
Churches often overlook the fact that they need to know exactly how many plates or baskets are being passed during the offering. It's a good idea to number each collection plate or basket. As you pass out plates to your ushers, keep a checklist for each service to verify which plates have been distributed. Before you begin counting the offering, verify that every plate or basket has been returned. Without this check and balance, a collection baskets can easily disappear without anyone realizing that it's even missing.

12. Is the handling of offerings always controlled by at least two people?

☐ Yes Notes _____
_____

☐ No _____
_____

Analysis
Handling of offerings

Even for churches that promote online giving or contributions made by check, many attendees will still drop cash into the weekly offering plate. Cash management procedures need to be established. The key word for handling cash is togetherness. At least two people need to be involved in every step of the cash receipts process. At least two people should collect the offerings, take the money to the counting area, count the offerings, and take the deposit bag to the bank. With the togetherness principle, only collusion between the individuals or extreme carelessness will cause problems. This control not only safeguards assets but also reduces the possibility that money handlers will ever be caught up in controversy.

13. Is the handling of other receipts of cash always controlled by at least two people?

☐ Yes Notes _____
_____

☐ No _____
_____

Analysis
Togetherness

Churches also receive cash from Sunday school classes, Mother's Day Out programs, preschool education programs, operations of schools, hot lunch programs, and so on. The togetherness principle for handling cash also applies in these activities. Thus Sunday school class secretaries and program directors should not unilaterally handle the cash generated in their respective areas.

14. Is cash counted in a secure area?

☐ Yes Notes _____
_____

☐ No _____
_____

Analysis
Secured area

Most churches have the offerings counted in a secured, locked room. Counting money in unsecured areas leaves cash susceptible to potential robbery. Churches that handle large sums of money also should consider using the services of armored vehicles to pick-up the Sunday offering for bank deposit so that these funds aren't left on the premises overnight or for an extended period of time.

Example 4.1: Check Endorsement

PAY TO THE ORDER OF
First National Bank

PORTER COMMUNITY CHURCH

FOR DEPOSIT ONLY
#946-24769

15. Do the money counters verify that the contents of the offering envelopes are identical to the amounts written on the envelopes by the members?

☐ Yes Notes _____

☐ No _____

Analysis
Verify collections

At least two money counters should open the envelopes, remove the contents, and compare the amount taken from each envelope with the amount written on the face of the envelope. If the amounts are not identical, the actual amount enclosed should be written on the envelope followed by the initials of the money counter. Large churches may have more involved procedures for handling such discrepancies.

Because the offering envelopes serve as the basis for posting to members' contribution records, they must be correct before being turned over to the bookkeeper or treasurer. It serves no purpose to deposit a sum of money that is different from the total shown on envelopes, which is posted to the accounting records. In fact, such a practice would automatically produce financial reports that do not balance.

16. Are all checks received restrictively endorsed as soon as possible?

☐ Yes Notes _____

☐ No _____

Analysis
Endorse checks

Using a rubber stamp to restrictively endorse all checks received is a sound internal control. An example of a restrictive endorsement is shown in Example 4.1. Using this protection, any checks lost or stolen cannot be cashed. Many churches have money counters endorse each check immediately after the amount is verified against the envelope.

17. Is cash deposited as soon as possible after receipt?

☐ Yes Notes _____

☐ No _____

Analysis
Speedy deposit

In most churches the offering is counted at the church and, within a few hours of collection, is deposited at the bank. Depositing funds as quickly as possible 1) lessens the risk of outright theft, 2) prevents the substitution of subsequently received receipts to cover shortages, and 3) increases the odds that the checks will be collectible. Yes, even churches encounter bad checks! Those churches waiting until Monday, Tuesday, or Wednesday to deposit Sunday's funds may be inviting trouble.

18. Is all cash received deposited in the bank?

☐ Yes Notes _____

☐ No _____

Analysis
Depositing cash

Cash receipts should be deposited *intact*, that is without being reduced by disbursements. Paying any expenses out of the available cash is a bad practice. As will be discussed later, all disbursements should be made by check or through the petty cash fund.

19. Is cash safeguarded in a safe, lock box, or similar protective container when at the church?

☐ Yes Notes _____
_____

☐ No _____
_____

Analysis
Securing cash

It is imperative that all cash be protected. The combination to the safe or the keys to the lock box should not be available to accounting personnel. Remember the importance of the separation of duties. A bookkeeper, for instance, who is responsible for taking care of the accounting records, and who also has access to the safe and lock box, is performing incompatible functions.

20. Are collection reports given to the bookkeeper or treasurer for entry into the accounting records and a copy sent to the internal audit committee for subsequent audit purposes?

☐ Yes Notes _____
_____

☐ No _____
_____

Analysis
Handling collections

Collections should never be handled by people who work with the accounting records. The counting committee should deposit cash in the bank and inform the record keepers of their activities. The optimum system for handling collections is as follows:

The counting committee counts the offerings and prepares a collection report indicating details of currency and coins, checks included in envelopes, and checks not included in envelopes.

The counting committee prepares the bank deposit slip in triplicate and deposits the monies in the bank. The original slip goes to the bank, one copy goes to the treasurer, and the other copy goes to the internal audit committee.

The collection report is also prepared in triplicate. The original, together with the opened envelopes, goes to the person in charge of recording contributions in the accounting records, a copy goes to the internal audit committee, and another copy is retained by the counting committee.

The entire collection-handling function is shown in Example 4.2. Although the process may seem complex, the only difference between the suggested approach and that currently followed in many churches is that extra copies of the deposit slip and collection report are required.

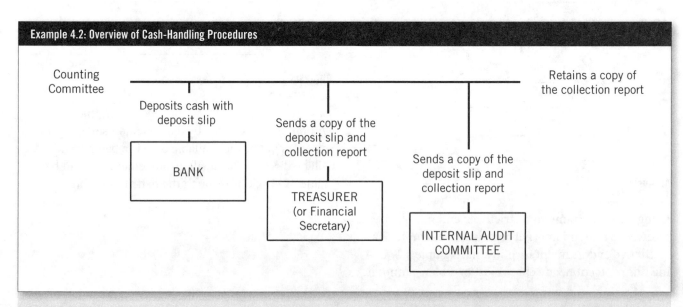

Example 4.2: Overview of Cash-Handling Procedures

21. Are incoming mail, in-office and electronic contributions handled by people who are not responsible for the accounting records?

☐ Yes Notes _____

☐ No _____

Analysis
Separation of duties
It would be foolish to install internal controls for the handling of the weekly offerings but neglect to install controls for midweek receipt of checks in the mail and in-office, and electronically received contributions. Yet many churches do just that, and a few have paid the price for their lack of controls. Establishing controls for these contributions is not easy; it might involve the use of some volunteers to achieve the necessary separation of duties.

To control cash coming in through the mail, someone who does not handle the accounting records should open the mail, prepare a list of the checks received, and deposit the money in the bank. That person should retain a copy of the list of checks together with a duplicate bank deposit slip. The original list of checks would be given to the financial secretary or treasurer. If a substantial number of checks are involved, the church should consider more elaborate controls. They may include having two people open the mail and forward copies of the receipts lists and deposit slips to the internal audit committee.

Other monies might also be received in the central church office and program offices as well. Members might stop by to make a special offering or restricted gift. Parents might come by to pay the tuition for their children enrolled in the church's programs. Senior citizens might pay for meals received. As with mail receipts, people handling the money should not handle the books. Some churches use pre-numbered receipts for cash received. This practice helps prevent cash from getting "lost."

22. Has the bank been instructed in writing never to cash checks payable to the church?

☐ Yes Notes _____

☐ No _____

Analysis
Cashing checks
It might surprise some people to learn that bank clerks can be talked into cashing an occasional check made out to the church. The perpetrator might build rapport with the bank clerk over a long period of time, and then one day say, "The pastor asked me to cash this check for him today instead of depositing it. He's going to visit a hospitalized member in Roseville." If the bank clerk follows the request, the church has lost some money. Of course, a letter to the bank might not prevent that situation from occurring. It does, however, fix the responsibility for the misappropriations with the bank.

23. Are contribution records maintained for members?

☐ Yes Notes _____

☐ No _____

Analysis
Recordkeeping
Keeping a record of members' contributions is a positive control because each member can compare his or her personal records against those of the church. It is now also required by the IRS to substantiate contributions.

24. Do all donors receive periodic (perhaps quarterly) notices of their contributions from the internal audit committee?

☐ Yes Notes _____
_____

☐ No   _____
_____

Analysis
Periodic notices

Sending members periodic notices is not only a control procedure but also a stimulus toward fulfilling pledges. Some churches use this opportunity to remind their members of their annual pledge, the amount given thus far, and the balance of the pledge. In other churches such a comparison would be impossible because pledges are either anonymous or are handled by a person or committee other than those responsible for recording receipts.

Regardless, periodic notices allow each member to compare his or her giving against the church's records. Errors and unusual lags in posting can be brought to the attention of the internal audit committee, which should be responsible for sending out the notices. Obviously, this process should not be handled by people responsible for the accounting records. The purpose of the procedure is to check on those involved with keeping the books.

25. Are members instructed to report any irregularities or errors in their notices of contributions to the internal audit committee?

☐ Yes Notes _____
_____

☐ No   _____
_____

Analysis
Reporting irregularities

Most churches do not tell members what to do if their contribution notices are incorrect. So what do most members do? They call the church office. And to whom do they talk? Often it is the person handling the accounting records. And what usually transpires? The person handling the records promises to check into the problem and send them a corrected statement. If any illegal scheme was being executed, all complaints could quickly be quieted by typing corrected notices and forwarding them to members without correcting the accounting records. This is one critical reason why it's important to let members know who to notify if there is a discrepancy in their record of giving.

INTERNAL CONTROLS: CASH DISBURSEMENTS

The following group of internal controls relates to the handling of cash disbursements in the church. The need for proper accounting controls for cash disbursements is as great as that for cash receipts. Whether it's coming in or going out, all cash needs to be properly handled and recorded.

Example 4.3: Purchase Order

St. Mark's Church **Purchase Order No. 1019**
245 Main Street   Date: 7/22/09
Anytown, IL 60643 Terms: 2/10, N/30

To: Outdoor Furniture Company
      741 Main Street
      Anytown, CA 90048

Ship To: Angels Camp, Route 49
          Anytown, IL 60643

Ship Via: **Truck**   Date Needed: **8/15/09**

Please accept our order for the following:

Quantity	Number	Description	Price	Per	Amount
20	T-1066	Picnic Table	$100	Table	$2,000

Note: Purchase Order number must appear on all shipping documents and invoices.

Order By *Tom Smith*

26. Are requisitions prepared for anticipated disbursements that do not have standing authorization?

☐ Yes Notes _____
_____

☐ No _____
_____

Analysis
Requisitions

In many churches, committee chairpersons, directors, activity leaders, and others can stop by or telephone the church office to request that something be ordered. The treasurer has the obligation to make sure that the order falls within the person's budget and, if so, that it is ordered, received, paid for, and charged to the correct account. These functions are not always executed properly because no organized system of purchasing or making payment has been established. Many churches operate with systems that are no more sophisticated than those used by individuals in their homes. Orders are placed without being documented; goods are received and paid for which were never ordered; goods are paid for twice; goods are paid for that have not been received.

Requisition form

The initial step in a purchasing system is the preparation of a requisition. Such forms can be purchased at office supply stores or can be generated by a business software package on a computer. Persons authorized to make purchases prepare the requisition, indicating the item or service they desire, reason for the request, estimated cost, vendor desired, and date needed. The original copy is sent to the financial secretary or treasurer, and a duplicate is retained by the preparer.

When the requisition is received, it is used to make sure that the good or service is both provided for in the budget and that the account to be charged has an adequate balance remaining. If both conditions are satisfied, the requisition is approved, and a purchase order is prepared. If both conditions are not met, the requisition is not approved, and the preparer is informed of the reason(s).

Although this procedure may seem cumbersome, it has several advantages. First, it keeps people from charging good and services to the church without approval. Second, this procedure keeps people from paying for items themselves and then presenting the receipt to the treasurer for reimbursement. Third, it allows the church office to select specific vendors. Some vendors may give the church a lower price, be especially dependable, or be members of the congregation or denomination. The person requesting the goods and services might not be aware of this.

Many expenditures, such as those for salaries, utilities, and mortgage payments, would have a standing authorization for payment. In such cases, requisitions and purchase orders would not be prepared.

27. Are pre-numbered purchase orders used for all disbursements that do not have standing authorization for payment?

☐ Yes Notes _____
_____

☐ No _____
_____

Analysis
Purchase orders

The use of purchase orders is an important internal control device for churches. Purchase orders should be used even if requisitions are not used. Many varieties of purchase orders are available at office supply stores or can be generated by computer software. Not only does the use of purchase orders provide structure and accountability for legitimate purchases, it prevents the possibility of the church being ripped off by the hordes of unscrupulous vendors who prey on churches. Knowing that churches tend to use volunteers and may not be as highly organized as profit-seeking businesses, some vendors will send unordered goods to churches. Schemes often involve supplies of some sort, like cleaning supplies or paper goods. The use of purchase orders will protect you from paying for unordered goods. If you receive such materials, you can contact the vendor and tell it where to pick up the merchandise. Without the use of purchase orders, you will always be uncertain whether the goods were really ordered.

An example of a purchase order is shown in Example 4.3. Note that the purchase order is pre-numbered and that the vendor is specifically instructed to place the number on all invoices and other shipping documents. No invoices should be paid unless and until vendors comply.

28. Are invoices for goods and services approved before payment is made?

☐ Yes   Notes _____

☐ No   _____

Analysis
Invoices

The company selling the merchandise or providing the service will send an invoice to the church for the amount involved. Often the invoice and the goods will arrive together or the invoice will be given at the time of the service. It is imperative that a person in authority approve the invoice for payment. This is best achieved by having the person who ordered the goods or services inspect what was received and sign the invoice. Only that person will know if the church received exactly what was ordered. The items could be the wrong color, size, quality, or so on. The church has no obligation to pay for anything that was not included on the purchase order.

29. Are invoices checked for accuracy before being paid?

☐ Yes   Notes _____

☐ No   _____

Analysis
Verify accuracy

All invoices should be checked for accuracy. The price, calculations, and terms of sale need to be verified before payment.

30. Is a check authorization stamp or slip prepared to support the disbursement of funds?

☐ Yes   Notes _____

☐ No   _____

Analysis
Authorization

Before a check is written, the treasurer must be certain that all steps in the cash disbursement system have been completed. Unauthorized disbursements have a way of occurring when the system is breached. A method to monitor all aspects of the system is to prepare a check authorization stamp or slip for each disbursement. An example of a paper slip is presented as Example 4.4. The slip has check-off spaces for the requisition number,

Example 4.4: Check Authorization

Check Authorization

Item	Number	Check When Approved
Requisition	546	✔
Purchase Order	1019	✔
Received		✔
Invoice	S-113	✔
Price		✔
Calculations		✔
Terms		✔
Approved By		✔
Receiver		✔

Approved for payment

Melinda Flowers

purchase order number, acknowledgement of receipt of goods or services, assurance of invoice accuracy, and approval for payment. An office supply store can create a similar form using a rubber stamp.

For online bill payments, and electronic funds transfers and wires, which are commonly used to disburse funds for overseas mission organizations, be sure you follow the same cash disbursement system shown in Example 4.5.

31. Are all disbursements of cash, except for minor items, made by serially numbered checks?

☐ Yes Notes _____

☐ No _____

32. Are there at least two signatures required for all checks?

☐ Yes Notes _____

☐ No _____

Analysis
Numbered checks
Almost all churches answer 'yes' to this internal control question. Pre-numbered checks are available at banks or business systems firms and also can be generated from computer software programs. A summary of the cash disbursement system recommended for paying bills is presented as Example 4.5.

Example 4.5: A Cash Disbursement System for Churches

- Prepare Requisition Slip
- Prepare Purchase Order
- Inspect Goods Received
- Check Invoice for Accuracy
- Prepare Check Authorization Slip
- Prepare Check

Analysis
Check signers
The protection that comes from having two persons responsible for signing checks is worth the extra effort involved. Without this control only one person is in charge of the cash, and, as we learned earlier, this increases the risk of financial missteps. Some churches even require three signatures on checks. Many churches authorize five people to sign checks, any two of whom will suffice for any check. This approach is wise because it considers the likelihood that some of the signers will be unavailable due to emergencies, vacations, or illness. Signature stamps should not be used in place of a real signature.

If the church has adequate resources to help, it is probably best not to have the treasurer be one of the check signers. If the treasurer signs first, implying that all supporting documents have been reviewed, few second signers will perform their duties carefully. Most will simply add their signature to the check, which of course violates the purpose of this internal control.

Signed blank checks
A final thought. What about the existence of signed blank checks in churches? Most individuals would not consider signing their own checks and leaving the rest of the check blank. Yet I believe I could walk into 30 percent of all churches during the summer months when their check signers are on vacation, and find a batch of signed blank checks! *This must not occur.*

If check signers are going on vacation, three possibilities exist. First, some bills can be paid early. Second, using estimates if necessary, checks can be prepared in advance for some bills and salaries. Estimated amounts can be corrected in later periods. Third, all disbursements by check can be stopped until the signers return. Creditors can be informed of the short delay; most will be understanding. Obligations to creditors must not supersede the church's obligation to protect its own assets. After all, this situation is typically of brief duration.

33. Do all check signers inspect all supporting documents before signing?

☐ Yes Notes _____
_____

☐ No _____
_____

Analysis
Inspect documents
Each person responsible for signing the church's checks should inspect all supporting documents before signing, regardless of who has signed before him or her. If, for example, two people must sign checks, there may be a tendency for the first person to sign without review, thinking that the second person will inspect the documents. Conversely, the second person may sign without review, relying on the first person's signature as evidence that a thorough review had taken place, especially if the first person is the treasurer, as mentioned above.

In situations where the two "signing inspectors" do not have equal experience, there might be a tendency for the junior person to become complacent if the documents have been inspected by the senior person. This should be avoided.

34. Are supporting documents canceled when checks are issued?

☐ Yes Notes _____
_____

☐ No _____
_____

Analysis
Cancel documents
A good practice is to cancel the supporting documents to a cash disbursement by stamping the invoice and any associated paperwork *"PAID."* Many churches also indicate the date paid and the number of the check issued. Such a practice reduces the possibility that the same invoice, or a duplicate, would be paid twice. Some church treasurers complain that vendors are quick to ask for payment but slow to respond when asked for a refund on a twice-paid bill. Also, many vendors do not have a policy of informing their customers of credit balances or of granting automatic refunds in cases of overpayment.

35. Are all voided checks marked and retained?

☐ Yes Notes _____
_____

☐ No _____
_____

Example 4.6: Petty Cash Voucher

Petty Cash Voucher

Date: _____

No. _____

Payee: _____

For: _____
_____

Amount: _____

Charge To: _____

Approved By: _____

Received By: _____

Analysis
Voided checks

All voided checks, regardless of why the voiding is necessary, need to be marked "VOID" with a broad felt pen and kept for reconciliation purposes. To maintain proper number sequence in the cash disbursements journal or checkbook, the check should be recorded, with a note that it was voided.

36. Is preparing a check to "Cash" prohibited?

☐ Yes Notes _____
_____

☐ No _____
_____

Analysis
Checks to "cash"

You might regularly write checks to "Cash" from your personal checking account, but checks prepared in this manner do not specify what the funds were used for. The church needs to know why every disbursement occurred, so preparing checks to "Cash" should not be permitted.

Some churches go further by prohibiting the issuance of checks made payable to a check signer and/or to the treasurer.

37. Are blank, unused checks safeguarded at all times?

☐ Yes Notes _____
_____

☐ No _____
_____

Analysis
Safeguarding checks

When checks are not being prepared, any blank, unused checks should be kept in a safe or lock box to prevent their theft and misuse.

38. Is a petty cash fund used for minor disbursements of cash?

☐ Yes Notes _____
_____

☐ No _____
_____

Analysis
Petty cash

Another important element in the control of cash is a petty cash system. A petty cash system establishes a fund that is used to make small payments, especially those that are impractical and uneconomical to make by check. Payments for minor items such as postage due, stamps, or small office supplies are examples of appropriate payments from petty cash.

A petty cash fund is created by cashing a check drawn on the church's regular checking account. The proceeds from the check are placed in a petty cash box that is controlled by a fund custodian. The custodian supervises the fund and is held accountable for any discrepancies. The fund should be adequate to cover payments for a short period – several weeks or a month.

39. Are vouchers prepared for all disbursements from the petty cash fund?

☐ Yes Notes _____
_____

☐ No _____
_____

Analysis
Vouchers

All payments for the petty cash fund should be supported with petty cash vouchers. A typical petty cash voucher is illustrated in Example 4.6. Each petty cash voucher indicates the date of the expenditure, the name of the individual receiving the money, the purpose of the expenditure, and the amount paid. Along with various invoices and receipts, petty cash vouchers are used as evidence of disbursements. When necessary and at the end of the accounting period, the petty cash fund should be replenished. At that time, the expenditures should be recorded in the accounting records.

40. Are transfers among bank accounts properly authorized?

☐ Yes Notes _____

☐ No _____

Analysis
Bank transfers
Most churches have several bank accounts. Transfers of funds between banks are typically done by check. But transfers of funds within a bank can be accomplished without preparing a check, without much paperwork, perhaps electronically, and possibly outside of existing internal controls. Funds may be moved from accounts with stringent requirements for disbursements to those with virtually no such requirements. Approval for all transfers should be required and documented in the accounting records, and transfers should only be allowed between church accounts. Sometimes there is no restriction and a person could transfer funds out of a church account into a personal account.

41. Are procedures in place to control the use of church credit cards?

☐ Yes Notes _____

☐ No _____

Analysis
Credit cards
Many churches have their own credit card(s). They are a convenient way to pay bills and raise less of a concern with the IRS in handling church ministry expenses. However, definite risks come with using church credit cards. Dangers include 1) not providing the treasurer with charge receipts, 2) personal charges made accidentally (or intentionally) on the church card, 3) cards being used for the convenience of church members or employees, not the church, 4) the ability to bypass the purchase order system described earlier, and 5) absence of any expenditure policies.

In addition to selecting and screening personnel as described earlier, churches need policies on the handling of the credit card and receipts, and they need to strictly enforce credit limits.

INTERNAL CONTROLS: RECONCILIATION PRACTICES

Several internal financial control practices relating to the reconciliation of accounts are recommended. Reconciliation involves comparing two records to determine if they agree. For example, you might have reconciled a cash register tape against the cost of each item purchased in a store to determine if you were overcharged.

42. Is reconciliation of all bank accounts prepared monthly by a person who is not involved in writing checks or handling cash?

☐ Yes Notes _____

☐ No _____

Analysis
Reconciling accounts
Reconciliation of bank accounts needs to be done monthly when bank statements are received. It is important that the work not be done by people who are involved in writing checks. Incidents have occurred when treasurers who prepare and sign checks are permitted to reconcile the bank accounts.

Bank statements should be mailed to a member of the internal audit committee or someone designated by the committee to reconcile the accounts. Monthly reconciliations should be retained for use during the yearly audit of the books.

Example 4.7: Bank Reconciliation

First Church
Bank Reconciliation
December 31, 20XX

Balance per bank statement		$10,000.00
Add receipts recorded on our books but not reported on the bank statement: December 30 deposit		1,500.00
		$11,500.00
Deduct disbursements recorded on our books but not reported on the bank statement:		
Outstanding checks —		
#777	$700.50	
#778	42.50	
#793	57.00	800.00
Adjusted bank balance		$10,700.00
Balance per church books		$9,400.00
Add receipt reported on the bank statement but not recorded on our books:		
Check deposited by Angela Rogelli to the church account		1,500.00
		$10,900.00
Deduct disbursements reported on the bank statement but not recorded on our books:		
Bank service charges	$10.00	
Check returned for insufficient funds	190.00	200.00
Adjusted book balance		$10,700.00

The reconciliation of bank accounts will uncover any items that appear only on the bank's books or only on the church's books because of 1) a timing difference, or 2) an error made by either the bank or the church. Common examples of timing differences follow.

Timing differences
Items might be recorded on the church books but not yet reported on the bank statements, such as:

- *Deposits in transit.* Deposits made near the end of the month may not be included on the bank statement. Deposits in transit are determined by comparing deposits listed on the bank statement with deposits recorded on the books.
- *Outstanding checks.* Checks may be written but not yet processed by the bank. Outstanding checks are determined by comparing checks reported on the bank statement against checks written on church records.

Items might be reported on the bank statement but not yet entered in the church's accounting records, such as:

- *Non-sufficient funds checks.* Members' checks might be returned because of lack of funds.
- *Bank service charges.*
- *Interest earned by the church and added to the account.*
- *Member contributions made directly to the bank.*

Errors
In addition to timing differences, errors might cause a discrepancy between the bank's recorded cash balance and the church's recorded cash balance. Bank errors might include charging the church's account for a check drawn by another bank customer, failing to record a deposit or transfer from another account, or entering an incorrect amount. Although the bank is typically larger than the church and uses the most sophisticated electronic equipment, banks make their share of mistakes. Bank statements should not be presumed to be correct until they are reviewed. Alternatively, church records could contain errors. Church errors might include incorrect addition on a deposit slip or an amount written on a check that is different from the amount recorded in the accounting records.

Several different types of reconciliations can be prepared. Most banks provide a reconciliation form with the monthly statements. A commonly used form allows the preparer to determine the amount of cash over which the church has control at a stated date. An example of such a bank reconciliation appears in Example 4.7.

The reconciliation deals with those items on the church's records and the bank's records that differ. The preparer considers these items and adjusts one cash balance or the other to bring both balances into agreement. In this case, First Church has an ending cash balance of $10,700 on December 31, 20XX.

Online banking
For many churches, online banking has become the primary means of managing funds. One major benefit of banking online includes having access to real-time reviews of bank accounts. Churches can check current balances and catch inappropriate transactions immediately instead of waiting for a monthly statement. With online banking, treasurers can review a bookkeeper's work at any point in time. Being able to log on any time, day or night, without having to tote financial records to and from the church office creates a much stronger internal control. Plus, online transactions generally are more secure than paper transactions. If you are still concerned about how to implement secure online banking, just ask to speak to a bank representative. He or she will discuss your questions and concerns.

Treasurers doing online banking on the church's or their own personal computer should:

- ☐ Make certain the website they are conducting church business on is secure before entering any data.
- ☐ Change passwords regularly.
- ☐ Shut down the computer when it is not in use or, at least, disconnect it from the internet.
- ☐ Monitor all bank activity very closely. If monies have been lost due to fraud, generally stated you have a 60 day window to get the funds refunded by the bank. Keep the security features of the computer software up to date, including the web browser, virus scan software, and firewalls.

- ☐ Never respond to unsolicited emails requesting validation of account information, so-called phishing.

43. Is the petty cash fund reconciled on a surprise basis at least once a year?

☐ Yes Notes _____

☐ No   _____

Analysis
Surprise reconciliation
A member of the internal audit committee or its delegate should periodically make a surprise visit to the petty cash custodian and ask to reconcile the fund. This means that vouchers for disbursements made from the fund would be added to the remaining cash to determine if all funds were accounted for. Therefore if the vouchers totaling $43 and coins and currency of $17 were found in the fund that should have $100, the fund would be short $40 [$100 − ($43+ $17)]. Because the custodian is responsible for the funds, some questions would need to be answered. Reconciling the petty cash fund is also a good time to see if vouchers are being prepared properly and if receipts and invoices are being saved.

44. Are account balances in the books ever reconciled with the amounts presented in financial reports?

☐ Yes Notes _____

☐ No   _____

Analysis
Reconciling accounts with reports
The end product of all the accounting functions is the preparation of financial reports for use in making decisions. If financial reports contain inaccuracies, faulty decisions could be made. The purpose of this control is to make sure that the accounting records are in agreement with the financial reports. There have been situations where embezzlement has been concealed by the embezzler preparing fictitious financial reports or where financial reports were wrong because the previous month's ending balance (the current month's beginning balance) was transferred incorrectly.

45. Are budgeted expenditures periodically reconciled to actual expenditures to ensure that funds are being spent as authorized?

☐ Yes Notes _____

☐ No   _____

Analysis
Reconciling expenditures
Treasurers need to be certain that expenditures are made as authorized in the budget by church leaders, not as unilaterally determined by a program director. For example, a youth director might be spending within his or her budget,, but might be buying unauthorized goods and/or services or might be conducting activities that have not been authorized by church leaders.

46. Are monies received as designated gifts to the church spent as directed by the donor(s)?

☐ Yes Notes _____

☐ No   _____

Analysis
Designated gifts
Designated funds have special attachments to them and should be disbursed for the specific purposes for which they were given. If designated funds are to be spent for items other than those for which they were designated, donors need to be contacted, given the opportunity to change their designation, or allowed to request that their monies be returned.

INTERNAL CONTROLS: OTHER ASSETS

Four final internal controls need to be introduced and discussed. These controls relate to the safeguarding of noncash assets.

47. Are valuables (i.e. securities, jewels, valuable documents) kept in a bank safe-deposit box?

☐ Yes Notes _____

☐ No   _____

Analysis
Safeguarding valuables
Valuables should be stored in a bank safe-deposit box. This is so that these assets, some of which might be used in religious ceremonies, can be protected from fire, theft, accidental loss or damage. Although a bank safe-deposit box is not usually free, it affords the church much better protection than even a safe at the church. The incidence of church robberies is far greater than that of bank safe-deposit box break-ins.

48. Are two signatures required for access to the safe-deposit box?

☐ Yes Notes _____

☐ No   _____

Analysis
Safe-deposit box
As with the handling of cash, no individual should be in a position unilaterally to control an asset. When only one person can get something from a bank safe-deposit box, good control is violated. Therefore two signatures should be required for entry into the bank's vault. Although this may seem cumbersome for those authorized to have access to the box, visits to the bank will probably be infrequent.

49. Is an updated inventory of securities, valuables, equipment, and other major noncash assets maintained?

☐ Yes Notes _____

☐ No   _____

Analysis
Annual inventory
An inventory of major noncash assets helps to verify the accountability for these kinds of assets, assists in determining if any assets are missing, and is valuable in case of fire or theft. All major items should be inventoried, ideally on an annual basis, whether in the office, sanctuary, kitchen, basement, or elsewhere.

The inventory record for each item should include at least the following: cost, date of acquisition, location, and description. If items have been retired from service, traded in, or sold, this should be noted on the inventory record.

Few churches maintain the type of inventory suggested and would, for example, be hard pressed to file an insurance claim for fire loss. This oversight is sometimes due to the cash-basis accounting approach used in most churches. When a church using cash-basis accounting pays for a piece of equipment, it appears as an expenditure of that year. Contrast this treatment with that in a business firm, where the same piece of equipment would be set up as an asset and depreciated each month. As a consequence of using cash-basis accounting, most churches do not monitor many of their assets after purchase. Existence and use of the asset is simply presumed. Maintaining adequate records of asset purchases will also be required in a church financial audit.

50. Are scheduled reviews made to determine if insurance coverage is adequate?

☐ Yes Notes _____

☐ No _____

Analysis

Insurance coverage

Insurance is obtained to protect the church's assets. But if no person or group is responsible for reviewing the adequacy of the coverage, the church might needlessly risk loss of assets. All insurance policies should be evaluated at least every two years. Suggested new coverage can be considered as necessary. A few churches appoint an insurance committee for this purpose.

Insurance should also be considered to protect the personal assets of those who serve the church. Consider directors' and officers' coverage to shield church officers and officials in the event that they are sued for actions committed, however tangentially, while they are serving the church. This insurance usually includes coverage for employment practices, liability for harassment, and discrimination suits. This is important because the comprehensive general liability policy which most churches have does not cover employment practices.

Let the lists you create based on your test score represent your short-term and long-term programs for the improvement of internal financial controls. Be the instrument of change!

For your convenience in sharing and discussing this test with others in the church, a summary list of the 50 internal financial controls is presented in Example 4.8.

■ ACTION ITEMS ■

☐ Discuss your church's test results. Are you surprised by the results?

☐ Which internal controls seem unnecessary for your church and why? Conversely, which controls do you think are the most important ones for your church to implement right away?

TEST RESULTS

Very few churches have a perfect score.
Now that you have reviewed all 50 internal controls, you are in a position to evaluate your church's overall system of controls. Don't fret if you failed to answer all 50 questions 'yes;' all is not lost! First, your church has plenty of company. Second, you now have sufficient information to make positive changes in your church.

To assist in your analysis, tally the number of 'yes' responses below for each category of controls discussed. You will quickly be able to tell which areas need special attention. Also, if you multiply your total number of 'yes' answers by two, you will be able to express your test results on a 100 percent basis. Thus, if you answered 'yes' for 26 controls, your church's score on the self-test would be 52 percent. This score would indicate that significant improvements should be made in your church's internal control system.

Internal Control for Churches

Type	Number Provided	Number 'Yes'
General	9	_____
Cash Receipts	16	_____
Cash Disbursements	16	_____
Reconciliation Practices	5	_____
Other Assets	4	_____
	50	_____

Now review all questions to which you answered 'no' and your accompanying notes. Indicate below those ten internal controls that can be easily implemented right now.

1. _____
2. _____
3. _____
4. _____
5. _____
6. _____
7. _____
8. _____
9. _____
10. _____

Next, in the space provided, list those ten internal controls that will take longer to implement but that are essential to protect the church's assets.

1. _____
2. _____
3. _____
4. _____
5. _____
6. _____
7. _____
8. _____
9. _____
10. _____

Example 4.8: Summary of 50 Internal Financial Controls for Every Church

General
1. Are facilities locked when not in use?
2. Does the church have a written, up-to-date accounting procedures manual?
3. Are the accounting records and the underlying internal controls audited annually?
4. Are the bookkeeper's or treasurer's activities limited to keeping the records of cash collections and preparing the support for disbursements?
5. Does your church's insurance policy include coverage for financial misconduct?
6. Do you utilize an internal audit committee?
7. Are new accounting personnel screened?
8. Has the church prepared an organizational chart for the accounting/financial area which is followed consistently?
9. Are the accounting records safeguarded at all times?

Cash Receipts
10. Are church members encouraged to give electronically, or to use offering envelopes?
11. Are collection plates or baskets numbered so you can verify that you have received all offerings?
12. Is the handling of offerings always controlled by at least two people?
13. Is the handling of other receipts of cash always controlled by at least two people?
14. Is cash counted in a secure area?
15. Do the money counters verify that the contents of the offering envelopes are identical to the amounts written on the envelopes by the members?
16. Are all checks received restrictively endorsed as soon as possible?
17. Is cash deposited as soon as possible after receipt?
18. Is all cash received deposited in the bank?
19. Is cash safeguarded in a safe, lock box, or similar protective container when at the church?
20. Are collection reports given to the bookkeeper or treasurer for entry into the accounting records and a copy sent to the internal audit committee for subsequent audit purposes?
21. Are incoming mail, in-office, and electronic contributions handled by people who are not responsible for the accounting records?
22. Has the bank been instructed in writing never to cash checks payable to the church?
23. Are contribution records maintained for church members?
24. Do all donors receive periodic (perhaps quarterly) notice of their contributions from the internal audit committee?
25. Are members instructed to report any irregularities or errors in their notices of contributions to the internal audit committee?

Cash Disbursements
26. Are requisitions prepared for anticipated disbursements that do not have standing authorization?
27. Are pre-numbered purchase orders used for all disbursements that do not have standing authorization for payment?
28. Are invoices for goods and services approved before payment is made?
29. Are invoices checked for accuracy before being paid?
30. Is a check authorization slip prepared to support the disbursement of funds?
31. Are all disbursements of cash, except for minor items, made by serially numbered checks?
32. Are there at least two signatures required for all checks?
33. Do all check signers inspect all supporting documents before signing?
34. Are supporting documents canceled when checks are issued?
35. Are all voided checks marked and retained?
36. Is preparing a check to "cash" prohibited?
37. Are blank, unused checks safeguarded at all times?
38. Is a petty cash fund used for minor disbursements of cash?
39. Are vouchers prepared for all disbursements from the petty cash fund?
40. Are transfers among bank accounts properly authorized?
41. Are procedures in place to control the use of church credit cards?

Reconciliation Practices
42. Are reconciliation of all bank accounts prepared monthly by a person who is not involved in writing checks or handling cash?
43. Is the petty cash fund reconciled on a surprise basis at least once a year?
44. Are account balances in the books ever reconciled with the amounts presented in financial reports?
45. Are budgeted expenditures periodically reconciled to actual expenditures to ensure that funds are being spent as authorized?
46. Are monies received as designated gifts to the church spent as directed by the donor(s)?
47. Are valuables (i.e. securities, jewels, valuable documents) afforded protection in a bank safe-deposit box?
48. Are two signatures required for access to the safe-deposit box?
49. Is an updated inventory of securities, valuables, equipment, and other major noncash assets maintained?
50. Are scheduled reviews made to determine if insurance coverage is adequate?

Chapter 5

Audits

by Vonna Laue

1. GENERAL OVERVIEW

One area that nearly all church leaders wish they could avoid is the audit. The word audit can instill fear in the hearts of even the most fastidious financial managers. Most people associate audits with the Internal Revenue Service (IRS).

For churches, though, there are several different types of audits—compliance audits performed by agencies such as the Internal Revenue Service (IRS) or the Department of Labor (DOL), internal audits using skilled volunteers in the congregation, and external audits or other levels of service performed by certified public accountants. In this chapter we will discuss the different kinds of audits churches may encounter—and what you'll need to know and do to avoid and prepare for one.

In many ways, audits are intended to help organizations. Even compliance audits, which are generally viewed as intrusive and fear-inducing, can actually net valuable information and insight into areas in which your church's financial team may need to improve.

The fiduciary responsibility of any organization lies with the chief executive, and in churches, this is the senior pastor. The senior pastor needs a solid understanding of the church's financial position and its financial reporting obligations. Although many pastors prefer not to get bogged down in these kinds of operational details, understanding the basics of each kind of audit will go a long way toward helping the church avoid certain audits while assisting in preparation for others. The church audit committee or board of directors has a fiduciary responsibility over the organization as well. Church boards often are ministry-focused and spend little time, or have little expertise, in the area of finances. In most churches the board will accept responsibility for overseeing both internal and external audits, but they will rely on their pastor for information and encouragement. Boards must also have an understanding of issues that may lead to compliance audits.

Noncompliance with government-established practices poses one of the biggest threats to a church's financial standing, and yet few churches understand many of the compliance requirements. In this next section, I will highlight the areas of compliance that are most significant for churches—the ones that create the biggest areas of liability and the stiffest penalties for noncompliance. This is a topic, however, that warrants more thorough training. I urge you to seek the counsel of a professional CPA to learn more about compliance requirements and to evaluate whether your church is following the correct measures to be in full compliance on these key areas.

2. COMPLIANCE AUDITS

There is a long-held belief that the IRS has no control over the actions of a church due to the Constitutional amendment protecting the separation of church and state. That understanding has been challenged in recent years, and more churches have found themselves under scrutiny for their tax returns.

Consider the following true example (fictitious names have been used to protect the identities of those involved):

> Bethany was asked to become the volunteer church treasurer for a relatively small congregation. She was a college student at the time and had little training, but was studying accounting in school and therefore was one of the more qualified and willing individuals in the church. She received a box of papers from the former church treasurer as he was moving out of town. The box contained miscellaneous information while the actual invoices and other documents were maintained in the church office.
>
> The time soon came for Bethany to pay the bills, so off to the church office she went. She asked Kimberly, the church secretary, where the bill folder was maintained. "It's in this drawer," Kimberly told her. Bethany opened the drawer and found not only the unpaid invoices, but also a file labeled "IRS." When Bethany asked Kimberly about the letters, Kimberly explained that she just put the unopened IRS letters in that folder whenever they arrived. To Bethany's dismay, she discovered that the letters related to correspondence regarding IRS Form 941 payroll reports, which the treasurer had never filed.

The former treasurer believed that churches were exempt from taxes and therefore were not subject to *any* IRS requirements. Bethany managed to correct the delinquent filings after extensive communication with the IRS. Finally, the church was able to move forward in full compliance with IRS regulations.

AVOIDING AN AUDIT

While a church's tax exempt status precludes it from some IRS regulations, there are many tax code regulations that *do* apply to churches. Churches that ignore these regulations do so at their own peril. Also, churches that satisfy IRS requirements are much more likely to avoid an IRS audit. Make sure you have the following items in order to try and avoid an investigation by the IRS:

- Treat paid individuals that receive payments properly as employees or independent contractors (see Example 5.2 for criteria)
- Withhold taxes properly from employee paychecks
- File the necessary forms (such as: quarterly 941 forms, year-end W-2 and W-3 forms, and annual 1099 and 1096 forms)
- Report unrelated business activity and pay all appropriate taxes
- Maintain adequate documentation to support positions that you take

Some inquiries by the IRS are the result of audits of individuals rather than the church itself. Records must be maintained in a way that assists staff and donors should their tax returns be examined. A record retention policy will help identify which records should be maintained and for what period of time. See Example 5.1 for a sample record retention policy. Keep in mind that the sample is a guideline and that retention cycles may vary.

A record retention policy should also include a document destruction policy. This provision determines how records that are older than the retention period should be destroyed and who is responsible for the destruction of those items. Record retention and document destruction policies were highlighted in the Sarbanes-Oxley legislation that was passed in 2002. Most non-profit attorneys believe the legislation has two requirements that relate to non-profit organizations including churches. The record retention and document destruction policy is one of those items.

It is a donor's responsibility to maintain records of their contributions. However, churches can help by providing accurate receipts that are in compliance with IRS standards. Receipts should include wording to inform the donor of any value of goods or services they received in return for their donation. The donor is only allowed to claim the excess amount as a charitable contribution. Current reporting requirements mandate donors provide bank records or written communication from the church to verify all donations made. Receipts can be issued after each contribution or on a regular basis (monthly, quarterly, or annually). Periodic statements should include detailed information on individual donations, especially those of $250 or more.

IRS guidelines also include information on how non-cash gifts are to be receipted (do not include the value of the gift on the receipt—that is the donor's responsibility—and specific forms that need to be submitted by the donor (Form 8282 and 8283). Richard Hammar's annual *Church & Clergy Tax Guide* (Your Church Resources/Christianity Today International) provides extensive information on how to substantiate charitable contributions.

The problem with excess benefits

Another area that can trigger an audit is excess benefit transactions. Churches have been under closer scrutiny in part because of the excessive salaries and compensation packages being paid to several high profile pastors. Maintaining adequate and appropriate compensation scales will also help the church to avoid potential investigations by the IRS. Churches that provide compensation packages that are out of line with industry standards are more likely to raise a red flag for the IRS.

Excess benefit transactions involve compensating an individual who is in a position of influence at a church beyond what their duties reasonably require. According to section 4958 of the tax code, any benefit provided by a tax-exempt organization to an employee that exceeds the reasonable value of the employee's services constitutes an "excess benefit transaction" that exposes the employee to substantial excise taxes (called "intermediate sanctions") of up to 225 percent of the amount that the IRS determines to be excessive compensation. This penalty only applies to "disqualified persons," who are officers or directors of the charity, or a relative of such a person. This compensation includes not just salary but all forms of payment or benefit that profits an individual, such as deferred compensation arrangements, housing and auto allowances, and medical reimbursement programs. Even one-time transactions can be construed as excess benefit.

On top of requiring a church to repay the excess benefit, the IRS also can impose an additional excise tax of 20 percent of the amount of the excess (up to a maximum penalty of $20,000, collectively.) As a result, if the imputed income is not reported as taxable income, it will constitute an automatic excess benefit under section 4958 of the tax code that will expose the pastor and board members (who approve the loan) to the excise taxes described above.

For this reason, compensation arrangements and other major financial agreements should be determined by a board of individuals unrelated to any individuals who might be affected by such decisions. Compensation decisions should be based on comparable data, such as that provided in the annual *Compensation Handbook for Church Staff* (Your Church Resources/Christianity Today International) and other employment-related resources by this publisher. All decisions should be documented in official minutes or church records in the event an IRS audit is required. You should always be able to provide documentation to support how you arrived at your compensation figures.

Department of Labor requirements

Besides the IRS, there are other agencies that require churches to follow specific regulations. The Department of Labor (DOL) is one such agency. Rules related to the Fair Labor Standards Act (FLSA) are monitored by this department. The primary concern for churches relating to the FLSA is the classification of employees and the payment of overtime wages. This is a major area of confusion and noncompliance for churches. Although a detailed study into this topic is beyond the scope of this book, church leaders would do well to learn all they can about the requirements of this act.

Briefly, employees can only be considered salaried (exempt) employees and not subject to overtime pay if they qualify under one of the following criteria:

- Executive – These individuals spend at least 50 percent of their time in management functions and directly supervise at least two full-time equivalents. They also must be able to make important decisions and typically would need to have the authority to hire and fire employees.
- Administrative – Typically, secretaries and administrative assistants will not be classified as exempt under this category. Individuals in this role will perform administrative duties but will have management functions as well and be empowered to make significant decisions without the requirement of additional approval from another supervisor.
- Professional – This category of exemption usually includes individuals whose work requires them to use judgment in the carrying out of their duties. Their positions are often considered intellectual careers and may involve ongoing licensing requirements, such as for teachers, accountants, and attorneys. Creative positions, such as writers, artists and musicians, and computer professionals may also be included in this category.

Exempt employees are typically paid a salary, which is not dependent on hours worked but rather on the job to be performed. For example, you can't tell an exempt employee that you will pay them a salary of $3,200 per month (an equivalent of $20 per hour for 160 hours) and then reduce their pay because they only worked 154 hours. If a salaried employee of the church takes a full day off, you can require them to use their paid leave for that day. However, if they work only a partial day, you cannot deduct a portion of their pay for the time missed.

If an individual is not considered exempt, they must be paid overtime when they work more than a certain number of hours in a day or week (this can also vary by the state in which your church is located). The risk you run with misclassification of employees and nonpayment of overtime is that the DOL could perform an audit and require payment of additional wages and penalties for underpayment.

There have been situations where church employees have kept track of the amount of overtime worked and later, when they were disgruntled and left their position (willingly or not), reported the church for underpayment of payroll and received significant amounts of back pay.

Another area to be careful of relating to employment practices in the church: one person filling two positions in the church—one salaried, the other non-exempt. In this scenario, you would be required to determine the potential exemption of each position based on its own merits.

Finally, be very careful of paid employees volunteering their time to the church. If they are volunteering in an area where they are employed, it will be very difficult to prove that you did not expect them to provide those services and therefore would be required to pay for them. Often, individuals will want to volunteer because of their dedication to the ministry. Have them serve in a role that is completely unrelated to their paid position.

Another practice that is widely—but mistakenly—used with non-exempt employees is providing compensatory (comp) time off instead of overtime pay. Tracking additional hours worked and "paying" in comp time is not a legal arrangement for a private employer, including churches. If a non-exempt individual has worked overtime, they must be paid for this time through payroll and not in other benefits such as additional time off.

SURVIVING AN AUDIT

I have touched on some of the main triggers for IRS and DOL audits relating to churches. If you still receive notification that your church will be audited, the best course of action is to be prepared! Have your records clearly in order. You should provide the information that is requested and comply with the auditors requests in a timely fashion. You will also want to consider engaging an accounting or law firm to assist with the audit process. They have expertise in these areas and can provide insight and support that will hopefully simplify and shorten the process.

Remember, ignorance is not a defense when it comes to compliance regulations. Every church needs to know the regulations that apply to them and follow them accordingly.

Two other kinds of audits are designed to create accountability and accuracy. First is one many churches perform regularly—an internal audit. Second, an external audit by an independent accounting firm provides excellent review of your church's records, reports, and internal controls. Let's start by looking at the benefits and procedures of an internal audit.

3. INTERNAL AUDITS

Internal audits are usually done for one of three reasons:

- Denominational requirement
- Church bylaw requirement
- Simply to be accountable

Many churches find an internal audit to be helpful in promoting goodwill among church members. Although there may be valid reasons why you would prefer not to have a church member examining the financial records of your ministry, often no disclosure is worse than full disclosure even when the church is dealing with a difficult matter. Plus, if you're not going to have an independent accountant perform an official church financial audit, an internal audit is the next best thing.

The purpose of this chapter is to help church volunteers who have provided their time and skills to assist the church in providing an objective assessment of the financial records. The information provided here will help your church begin—or improve—an internal audit process.

An internal audit should be done annually but not less often than every two years. It is difficult to look for discrepancies and find patterns when the internal audit procedures are performed inconsistently.

The governing board or a designated committee (i.e. finance committee) should determine the extent of procedures the internal auditor will perform. This should be clearly communicated. Items to consider would be:

- On what basis will the financial statements be considered–cash or accrual?
- When will the procedures take place?
- Are there any areas of particular importance?
- Who will the reports be given to?

An internal audit can generate several different outcomes. Ideally, two reports should be created. The first report should address the questions and concerns relating to staff and administration. This report should outline what the internal auditor had been asked to perform and the results of those procedures. If the auditor has discovered ways to improve the financial record keeping and reporting, he or she should convey these suggestions to the staff. The internal auditor should remain unbiased and helpful. It is NOT the internal auditor's responsibility to implement, or oversee the implementation of, any suggestions.

The internal auditor should also prepare a less-detailed report to share with the congregation. The board can determine what form they would like this report to take. Often it includes a summary of the audit process, but it would not include suggestions for improvement. While the church wants to be open in their communication, providing information related to suggestions without the context or communication that the board and management will have received could lead to confusion and unnecessary frustration.

ST. CHAOS UNDERGOES AN INTERNAL AUDIT

Let's revisit St. Chaos. They have learned from the difficulties encountered on their journey documented in this book. There is a strong desire to do things right. Now that the budgeting process has been implemented properly and they are monitoring things better, they are ready to move on to an accountability stage.

The finance committee and staff agreed that they weren't ready or able to hire a CPA for an external audit. They would like to get to that point sometime, but for now they have decided to do an internal audit. A volunteer at the church who has experience preparing for external audits at his workplace agrees to perform an internal audit for St. Chaos. Here are the steps St. Chaos will need to take to embark on an internal audit:

To begin the internal audit process, the staff should prepare items to be reviewed just as if an external auditor was performing the process. See the sample internal audit preparation list at Example 5.5. Here is a series of procedures that internal auditors should consider:

General information

- Obtain a trial balance report for the year under examination. Scan the report for any unusual items and make sure that the report balances to $0 (debits equal credits). If not, the bookkeeper will need to follow up on the error and may need to consult with an accounting consultant or with the software company.
- Review minutes of the board meetings (trustees, directors, etc.) as well as minutes from committee meetings, such as finance and personnel, to determine if there are any financial decisions that should be reflected in the financial statements.
- If the financial statements are accounted for under the accrual basis of accounting, discuss if there were any appeals made to the congregation that would require commitments to be recorded as pledges receivable.
- Review the processes for each area of accounting. This would include the various cash receipts areas, cash disbursements, and payroll.
- Look at existing contracts and commitments including leases and debt agreements to determine if they are properly reflected in the financial statements.
- Review a sample of expense reports and corporate credit card charges to determine that they meet the accountable reimbursement plan requirements of the church and that adequate supervisory approval has been obtained. This area is of particular importance to a church. If someone makes an accusation of misspent funds, it is very helpful to have reviewed these expenses in detail each year to protect the individual as well as the entire ministry.
- Check to make sure that all accounts are recorded in the general ledger. Often, a church will have

separate accounts that are not considered part of the general fund and therefore, are not included in the financial records of the church. They need to be included though. If there is a missions fund or if a ministry, such as women's ministry or youth ministry, maintains a separate bank account under the employer identification number of the church, those funds and activities must be included in the financial accounting of the church.
- Obtain a statement of financial position and statement of activities. Compare the financial statements with the supporting information obtained in the detailed testing discussed in the following pages.
- Have management prepare an analytical comparison of the current year account balances with the prior year. This analysis should include an explanation of any significant differences. The internal auditor can determine that threshold. For example: percent variances of ten percent and a dollar variance equal to one percent of total revenue (e.g. $2,500,000 of total revenue would yield explanations for differences greater than ten percent and $25,000). The internal auditor would review those explanations and determine if they seemed reasonable. If contributions increased 25 percent during the year, but the internal auditor knew that attendance was down 15 percent and many in the congregation were impacted by the poor economy, more testing may be necessary.
- Consider if a variance analysis between budget and actual amounts would also be helpful to the internal audit process. The governing board or a subcommittee often reviews this in detail monthly and additional analysis may not be significantly beneficial.

Here are some specific testing suggestions based on the account balances of the church:

Cash

Every church should have some cash! This is the lifeblood of every organization. The cash account has the most activity and is one of the most susceptible to accounting errors and internal control deficiencies. Internal auditors should note the following items:

- Review the bank reconciliations.
- Verify that the bank statement amount on the reconciliation is the same as the amount on the actual bank statement.
- Verify that the general ledger or "book" amount on the bank reconciliation is the same as the amount on the trial balance for that account. Some software will perform a reconciliation with selected transactions but not with the entire account activity. Reconciling this balance to the trial balance report will determine if there are any discrepancies.
- If there are large outstanding checks or deposits in transit, select a sample to agree with the next month's bank statement to be sure they cleared timely.
- Look for other large or unusual reconciling items. Sometimes a reconciliation will include a line labeled "Miscellaneous Adjustment" or something similar. If it seems unusual, follow up.
- If the reconciliation is done manually, or outside of the accounting software, be sure that the calculations were done properly. Remember, it's like elementary school. If someone forgets to carry one number, the whole problem is wrong!

Items to watch for or report to the board:
- If there are no bank reconciliations, this is a definite sign of potential problems within the church finances.
- Are there old outstanding checks that have not cleared? Should some of the checks be voided and reissued? Your state may have an unclaimed property law and require that funds be submitted to the state on behalf of those individuals.
- If there are large outstanding deposits, it's unlikely that they will clear. Banks usually deposit funds within twenty-four hours. It is probable that an error was made and needs to be corrected for the financial activity to be properly reported.
- Does it appear some checks may have been printed in the current year and back dated to the prior year either for budget purposes or to artificially decrease the accounts payable balance? This is usually noted when a large number of outstanding checks are dated around the end of the fiscal year.

- Are there unusual reconciling items? This can be the result of poor record keeping or potentially even fraudulent activity.

Investments

Many churches have limited investment activity. Many smaller churches will have a brokerage account available should a donor want to contribute appreciated stock to the ministry. This is often liquidated immediately and the cash is deposited in the primary bank accounts of the church. If an organization has substantial investment activity, it is probably beyond the scope of a volunteer internal auditor. However, for those churches with limited activity, a sample of procedures is included here:

- Review the investment policy to determine if the organization has complied with the policy.
- Reconcile the broker statement to the general ledger account balance.

Items to watch for or report to the board:
- If there is no investment policy, one should be drafted and approved by the board. It may be as simple as "investments received as contributions will be liquidated immediately and no investments will be carried by the organization."

Accounts Receivable

Typically, a church will have limited or no accounts receivable. All ministry activity including retreats and youth events are usually paid for before they take place. Trying to track accounts receivable for these types of activities would be very time consuming and probably have little impact. As the service would have already been provided, the attendee would have little motivation to pay the amount due and amounts collected would likely be small.

Churches that operate some form of school such as preschools or elementary schools will have accounts receivable activity. If there are accounts receivable, here are a few key items to review:

- Look at the detailed listing of accounts receivable and make sure that the total ties out to the general ledger account balance.
- When reviewing the detail, identify the account balances that are old and find out if they are still collectible.
- Ask staff what the policy is for collecting outstanding balances and what measures are taken before writing off accounts.

Items to watch for or report to the board:
- Excessive accounts receivable balances that are old and likely uncollectible.
- If there are no formal collection procedures in place, a procedure should be developed.

Notes Receivable

Few churches will have notes receivable. There will be some ministries that decide it is in the best interest of the church and the staff to provide a note receivable for senior staff in the purchase of a home or for other reasons. The church is not in the banking business and this should be minimal. The following procedures should be performed if there are notes receivable recorded in the general ledger:

- Find out if your church has determined that such notes receivable are legal and allowable in the state where the church is located. Several states have regulations related to this type of activity.
- If there are notes receivable with senior staff, ask the finance committee or church board to verify that an assessment has been completed to determine if the activity could be considered an excess benefit transaction for the individual. If so, there could be significant tax penalties for the individual and possibly for others in management or on the governing board.
- Review board minutes approving any new notes receivable with senior staff.
- Review a listing of the notes receivable and verify that they agree with the balance.
- Verify that payment terms are current.
- Determine if any notes are non-interest bearing. If so, interest is to be imputed for proper presentation of financial statements in accordance with generally accepted accounting principles.

Churches that have financial statements presented on a modified cash basis may not be concerned with imputed interest, but the interest that is not charged and any forgiven debt must be included as taxable income to the individual and reported on all appropriate payroll filings.

Items to watch for or report to the board:
- Any notes receivable to management that were not approved by the board
- Any noncompliance or unknown compliance with federal or state requirements, such as loans to officers or management of the church or tax consequences, such as excess benefit transactions or unreported income

Property and Equipment

An internal auditor will only review this information if the church maintains their financial statements under the accrual basis of accounting. Property and equipment may also be referred to as fixed assets. Many churches will record some assets but may not include all of them. Others may not record depreciation. This probably results in more misleading information than if no items were presented at all. If property and equipment are presented in the financial statements, the following items would be considered during the internal audit process:

- Review the policy for capitalizing fixed assets. The policy should include what the qualifications are for treating the purchase as an asset rather than an expense, such as a dollar threshold and how long the asset will be used.
- If procedures require approval by the board of purchases over a certain dollar amount, review the board minutes to verify that the appropriate approval was obtained.
- Review the detailed list of property, equipment, and depreciation and verify that it agrees with the general ledger balances.
- Find out if there are any assets that have been purchased that are not included in the listing or if there are any items on the listing that are no longer used by the church.

Items to watch for or report to the board:
- Any discrepancies noted between the policy and the implementation of the policy.
- Any items that were purchased without the appropriate approval.

Inventory

More churches have inventory now than was common ten years ago. This inventory is primarily related to auxiliary operations such as bookstores or cafes. An internal audit would focus on the follow items related to inventory:

- Reconcile the detailed list of inventory with the general ledger balance.
- Review the listing for items that may be obsolete (not able to be sold or will be sold below the inventoried cost).
- Find out if inventory counts are performed and how significant the adjustments were as a result of the differences.

Items to watch for or report to the board:
- Significant amounts of obsolete inventory.
- If there are no physical inventory counts performed.

Accounts Payable and Accrued Expenses

Obligations of the ministry should be reported in the financial statements unless those statements are presented on a cash basis only. The information presented is very useful for management and the board to make educated decisions about operations and future ministry opportunities. If there are large amounts of payables or accrued expenses, it significantly impacts the future cash flows of the church. It is crucial for the integrity of the ministry to pay vendors and creditors in a timely fashion. Tracking this information in the accounting records will allow leaders to determine if this is happening. Internal auditors should perform the following procedures:

- Review the listing of accounts payable and determine that it agrees with the general ledger balance.

- Review the listing of accounts payable and determine that the amounts are not significantly past due.
- Inquire if there are other accrued expenses such as payroll liabilities that have not been paid and if they are properly reflected within the general ledger as well.

Items to watch for or report to the board:
- Outstanding amounts owed that are significantly past due.
- Any accrued liabilities that were not previously reported in the financial records that should have been.

Deferred Revenue

If an organization has accounts receivable, they may have deferred revenue as well. They may have deferred revenue even if there are no receivables but these two accounts are related to each other. Deferred revenue is recorded when funds are received in advance of services being provided. Deferred revenue for a church is often the result of an upcoming event that has a charge associated with it, such as a concert or a retreat. Funds are recorded as a liability by the church until the corresponding event occurs at which time the funds are released from the liabilities and recorded as revenue to the ministry. Deferred revenue also exists for school operations when tuition is received in advance of the period in which it is earned. The following are some steps for an internal auditor to test deferred revenue balances:

- Determine if there are events which would potentially produce deferred revenue.
- Review a listing of deferred revenue amounts and reconcile them to the general ledger balance.
- If the internal auditor has concerns about the balance being correct, they may want to look at some of the deposits prior to year-end and determine if the amounts were properly recorded as revenue or deferred revenue.

Items to watch for or report to the board:
- Amounts inappropriately reported as revenue instead of deferred revenue.
- Old deferred revenue amounts that may need to be refunded (amounts received for a trip that was indefinitely suspended).

Notes Payable

Many churches have incurred debt to a financial institution for various reasons. Often it was to expand their operations. This debt needs to be reflected in the accounting records properly. An internal auditor will perform certain activities such as the following to test those balances:

- Reconcile the bank statement to the general ledger balance.
- Determine that the interest expense recorded is approximately correct based on the review of the bank statements.
- Review the loan documents and information provided by the accounting staff to determine that the church is in compliance with all loan covenants. Failure to comply with loan covenants can result in the loan being called by the bank and being fully payable within a short time frame.
- If there are notes payable to individuals or organizations that are not financial institutions, be certain that those agreements are lawful and have been approved appropriately. Also, make sure that all interest paid is reported properly to the individuals including the completion of any necessary forms such as 1099-INT forms.

Items to watch for or report to the board:
- Non-compliance with debt covenants.
- Non-compliance with reporting standards.
- Any notes that have not been approved by the church. This may seem unlikely. However, some church leaders have been known to take on debt for the ministry, such as a line of credit to cover operating losses or other poor financial decisions, without the knowledge or approval of their governing board or leadership teams. This is obviously detrimental to the finances of the church as well as trust within the organization.

Net Assets (Equity)

The equity section of a church is very different from that of a for-profit corporation. While we will not discuss the specific accounting requirements in this chapter, there are a few things in particular that an internal auditor should pay attention to. They include the following:

- Are there any permanently restricted amounts, including endowments, that have been established.
- Are all temporarily restricted amounts properly identified? If an individual gives money for a specific purpose and that purpose has not been fulfilled yet, the balance needs to be separately identified so that church staff and the board know that these are not available for operations.
- Are any board-designated amounts properly reflected? Some boards will require reserves to be maintained for various events, such as for the repair or replacement of major items like HVAC equipment, or the cancellation of weekend services due to weather. Cancellations can greatly effect a ministry's fnances, especially if a service is cancelled on a weekend that typically generates larger offerings, like the first Sunday of the month. Having a board-designated reserve for these situations can help avert these kinds of financial crises. Designated amounts should be reported so they also are not factored into the general operations of the church.

Items to watch for or report to the board:
- Any amounts that were not previously reported that should have been.

Revenue

The primary source of revenue for a church is contributions. Other revenue may include things like interest income and revenue from various programs of the church. Internal auditors will perform procedures like those detailed below to test these account balances.

- Reconcile the total contributions from the donor system to the general ledger balance.
- Review any reconciliations that may have been performed for program revenue. Include analytical information, such as the number of students enrolled in the school times the tuition rate, or the attendance at concerts times the ticket prices to reconcile to program revenue.
- Find out what the processes for receiving cash in various departments is within the church and determine if the controls appear adequate.

Items to watch for or report to the board:
- If reconciliations of revenue accounts are not taking place.
- If cash is being received by various departments without adequate controls over those funds.

Expenses

The largest expenses of a church are typically related to personnel and facilities. It is important that all expenses are recorded and that they are recorded properly. An internal auditor would perform procedures similar to the ones detailed below.

- Reconcile Form 941 reports for the year to total expenses. Recognize that there are reconciling items such as housing allowances which are not taxable income on the Form 941 but may be included in the salary expense accounts of the church.
- Review the listing of expenses and look for any unusual items. For example, is there a miscellaneous expense account that has $25,000 in it? The internal auditor should review the general ledger detail of any items that seem questionable. Individual invoices may need to be examined if there are still uncertainties about the appropriateness of the expense.
- If the church prepares their financial statements in accordance with the accrual basis of accounting, review the detail of any large repairs and maintenance accounts or accounts that appear to be related to equipment or other property type items. Large amounts included in the detail should be questioned to determine that they were appropriately expensed and should not have been capitalized as an asset on the statement of financial position.

- Items such as depreciation expense and interest expense will have been verified in testing referred to previously such as property and equipment and notes payable.

Items to watch for or report to the board:
- Payroll items that appear to be handled incorrectly
- Any unusual items that were not resolved in the detailed review of expense accounts and subsequent communication with management

With this suggested internal audit plan, the volunteer internal auditor at St. Chaos should be able to prepare a report that will present good feedback on the financial information that is being provided currently, as well as some suggestions on areas where improvement may be needed.

There are times when an internal audit will not be sufficient. If there are significant differences of opinions within the congregation or there are sensitive issues, it may be time to call in an independent auditor. Also, some churches engage in activities that create complex tax and reporting requirements. Examples of these activities include:

- Trusts and annuities (held by the church as trustee or an outside organization)
- Pension liabilities
- Self-insured benefit plans
- Alternative investments (assets without readily marketable values, such as hedge funds or real estate funds)
- For-profit activities
- Large peripheral ministries (school activities, seminaries, missions sending programs, etc.)

Complex scenarios like these require specialized accounting knowledge, which may be beyond the scope of what a volunteer internal auditor can handle proficiently. Churches are wise to bring in independent, qualified professionals to help audit and provide accounting services to manage these complex activities.

4. EXTERNAL AUDITS

There are various levels of service that independent accountants perform for churches. Before we look at why and how to do an external financial audit, let's look at two other steps churches can take before embarking on a full-fledged financial audit.

The first is a compilation. This is simply the preparation of your financial statements, usually including the statement of cash flows and footnotes. While accountants are required to research any obvious errors, this level of service provides no formal assurance that your books are in order.

The second level of service is a professional review. This review involved answering questions and providing explanations of variances to the accountant along with providing some limited documentation. A review is the "tell me" engagement. It will involve answering questions and providing explanations of variances to the accountant along with providing some limited documentation.

Where the professional review is the "tell me" engagement, an audit is the "show me" event. Auditors will review records thoroughly and be required to follow-up on inquiries rather than just rely on your word. This level of audit can only be performed by certified public accountants.

Why would your church have an audit? This is a good question, and there are several reasons for choosing to have an audit performed. These include:

- Lender requirements. Sometimes covenants associated with debt will require an independent audit or review.
- The bylaws of your church may require an audit. Do you know if yours does?
- Involvement of an independent expert certainly lends credibility to the financial statements of the church.
- If your church is a member of an accountability organization, an audit may be required.

- Some donors or foundations require an audit report before giving large gifts.

Ideally, your auditor will work with you as a ministry partner. You'll want to select an audit firm that has experience working specifically with churches to help insure that they understand your ministry vision and goals. The auditor is not hired to "get you." You are willfully choosing to lean on their expertise. Not only should you view this experience as an opportunity to improve, you should encourage your staff to reap the benefits of the process. Following are some suggestions for making the most of the audit engagement.

BEGINNING THE PROCESS

The board needs to be involved, along with management, in the audit process. A request for proposal is sent to the audit firms that you would like to receive a proposal from. The request would typically include or request the following information:

- The period to be audited
- A proposed time frame for the audit work completion
- The proposed fee for the engagement, including expenses and the rates of additional services during the year
- A deadline for when the proposals are to be received by the church
- An understanding of the audit staff that will be involved in the engagement and their expertise in the field of church accounting
- Provide information on who the auditing firm should contact with questions or to schedule a meeting in advance of preparing the proposal

SELECTING AN AUDITOR

Church auditors should be considered carefully before selecting one to perform your church's audit. Here are some items to consider in the selection of an independent accounting firm:

- Does the firm have extensive experience with church audits?
- Obtain a copy of the firm's most recent peer review. This is the "audit" of the auditors and will help you determine the quality of the work they perform.
- Have the firm describe the audit procedures they perform, the timing of the work to be done, and how they will work with you to prepare for the audit.
- If this is a new audit firm for your church, gain an understanding of how the first year charges will be handled. Some firms will charge additional amounts the first year because of the hours required and some will factor that in as a cost of doing business in a long-term relationship.
- Review the references provided by the audit firm. Inquiring of those churches can be helpful. The firm will likely only give you clients they believe are satisfied. However, there may be issues that the reference church identifies as not important to them in which the firm's services are not as adequate as they would like and those services may be very important to you.

Once selected, the auditors will provide an engagement letter which is the contract. This document should be reviewed by both management and the board, but the board (or a designated committee, such as the finance or audit committee) should sign on behalf of the church. The auditors are ultimately responsible to the governing board. The American Institute of Certified Public Accountants recommends that you review the engagement letter for several items including the following:

- Description of the services to be performed (i.e. audit)
- Timetable for services to be completed
- Fees to be charged (including out-of-pocket expenses)
- Payment terms
- Written acceptance by the church

PREPARATION FOR THE AUDIT

The auditors will provide a preparation list requesting multiple items that will be obtained or reviewed during the time of the actual audit fieldwork. A sample of a preparation list is included as Example 5.3. Many of these items are much easier to prepare if work is done throughout the year and not just at year-end. A well-designed and implemented monthly closing process will make the audit preparation less of an "event" and more of a routine process. A sample closing checklist is also included as Example 5.4.

The timing of the audit is very important for you, your staff, and the auditors. You will want to determine your expectations and work closely with the auditors to find a mutually acceptable timeframe for each of the deadlines such as when the planning work will be done, when the final fieldwork will be completed, and when the final audit report will be delivered. Many of these dates will depend on outside parties such as trustee board meetings and loan covenant deadlines. Scheduling the audit is just one indication of how important good communication is between churches and their independent auditors.

It is crucial for a church to take an audit seriously and invest the necessary time and resources for it to be a positive process for the church and the auditors. It is a somewhat disruptive process because of the preparation time required as well as the time required during the auditors' fieldwork and the wrap-up questions after they have been on-site. The time that you invest in the preparation will save you a significant amount of time later. In the spirit of providing adequate time and resources, you should plan vacations of employees and management that are involved in the audit such that they will not interfere with the preparation and completion of the audit.

Review the preparation list when you receive it and determine how much time it will take to prepare the necessary items. Be sure to be realistic. This is not something that you look at the day before the auditors are scheduled to arrive.

Audit standards

Your church should stay current regarding new accounting pronouncements. Your auditors can provide information to you and help you understand the implications of new standards in relationship to your financial statements.

Audit fieldwork

Many of the procedures are similar to the internal audit. However, an external auditor will likely be more thorough and require more information in each of the areas as they test the balances and agree amounts to the trial balance. Keep in mind that additional external verification will be required. The external auditors will verify account balances with independent sources such as banks or brokers.

The length of time it takes to complete an audit can vary significantly. Obviously, the size of the church operations factor in to the amount of time spent in the audit process. The timing can also be somewhat dependent on the individual audit firm. A very general estimate would be to plan for the auditors to spend three days doing preliminary procedures and planning the final audit engagement. This would usually take place sometime around your fiscal year-end (slightly before or after). The auditors will schedule the final fieldwork with you and that would be approximately one week on-site at your church within a few months after your year-end. The auditors will then have procedures that they need to do after they leave your facilities. These steps include a quality control process. Once the audit work is completed, a draft of your audit report will be prepared and presented to you.

MANAGEMENT COMMENT LETTER

An audit report includes the auditor's opinion, the financial statements, and the footnotes. However, an auditor will also provide a management comment letter. This is a document intended solely for the use of the board and management. It is a way for auditors to communicate items required by the audit standards, but the primary focus for you should be the valuable information it provides to help your ministry. This letter should not be seen as a poor reflection on the church or the administration department or a report of things that were done wrong. Rather, it should be viewed as an opportunity to improve. Some would see this as the most important part of the audit.

Comments in the management comment letter are typically segregated in to three categories. First, material weaknesses are those weaknesses in the financial systems that are likely to result in a material misstatement to the financial statements. Second, significant deficiencies are issues that are likely to cause a significant, but not material, misstatement to the financial statements. Finally, other current year matters will include items that are not expected to have a significant impact on the financial statements. The last category will typically include best practices or items that may impact employees but may not have a financial impact on the organization. Samples of comments you may see in a management comment letter include *(standard categorization included in parentheses)*:

- Documentation of internal controls—New auditing standards consider inadequate documentation of the components of internal control to be at least a significant deficiency, and possibly a material weakness. We recommend that management perform a risk assessment as related to the financial statements and document the risks and related mitigating controls for the most substantial risks. *(material weakness or significant deficiency)*
- Monitoring—New auditing standards also consider inadequate oversight and monitoring of the internal controls to be at least a significant deficiency and possibly a material weakness. We understand the finance committee is actively involved in overseeing the financial operations of the church. We recommend that the board and/or finance committee begin looking at ways to improve its ongoing monitoring to include the area of internal controls. *(material weakness or significant deficiency)*
- Excess benefit transactions—It was noted during the audit that the compensation of the pastoral and executive leadership team is not reviewed for reasonableness with comparable data. Because of the possibility of severe penalties if compensation is determined to be excessive by the IRS, we recommend that the church adopt a policy whereby all management level employees' salaries are approved based on comparable data and that all forms of compensation be included in that assessment. *(other current year matter)*
- Management has not established the proper segregation of duties over cash receipts, cash disbursements, and payroll. For example, the same person prints, signs, and mails checks as well as receives and reconciles the bank statement. We recommend that each of the processes be reviewed and determine where additional individuals may need to be involved. Volunteers in the congregation may be able to provide additional support to mitigate these risks if the staff size is limited. *(material weakness)*
- Benevolence policy – Funds received for benevolent purposes must be handled carefully. Churches need to be certain that tax-deductible donations are not personal gifts, rather that they are given to a benevolence fund and distributed based on criteria established by the church. Benevolence requests will typically be made to a small group and the need considered as well as the availability of funds. We recommend that the church adopt formal, written policies governing the use of benevolent funds. *(typically other current year matters)*
- Expense reports and corporate credit cards—We reviewed a sample of the corporate credit card charges and reimbursed employee expenses and noted that some lacked either adequate documentation of ministry purpose, substantiation (including receipts), or proper approval. We recommend the church adopt and adhere to a formal accountable reimbursement plan to avoid the taxability of payments to employees. *(other current year matters)*

Sometimes the comments will not have a direct financial effect. As discussed earlier, you should be seeking a ministry partnership in your engagement of the auditors. With significant experience in the "church world," auditors will often have recommendations that may seem outside the scope of the audit. The management comment letter is a confidential document where recommendations can be made. Certainly, there will be informal communication throughout the process. This letter is a way to make the board or finance committee aware of potential concerns as well. If those individuals feel the comments are unwarranted, they can certainly address that with the auditors before the letter is finalized.

AFTER THE AUDIT

You will review the financial statements in a draft form provided by your auditor. When you review the drafts, you should consider the following:

- Is the audit opinion unqualified? This means that there were no limitations placed on the auditor and that they were able to determine that the financial statements were materially correct.
- Does the format of the information help your readers (management, board, congregation, etc.) understand the financial operations of the church?
- Is the information correct – does it agree with your general ledger after you have recorded any adjusting journal entries provided by the auditor?
- Is the information in the footnotes accurate and do you understand it?

If the answer to any of the previous questions is no, you need to clarify your understanding with the auditor. Keep in mind that the only portion of an audit report that belongs to the auditor is the opinion. All of the financial and footnote information is the representation of the church.

The draft reports need to be reviewed by those responsible for the process which would consist of the business administrator and executive pastor and others hopefully to include the senior pastor and finance committee or governing board. Any questions should be directed to the auditors and resolved prior to giving final approval of the reports. Those at the church responsible for the audit will be required to sign a representation letter. This letter indicates that all information has been provided or disclosed to the auditors so that they were able to make an appropriate determination of the reasonableness of the financial statements.

BOARD PRESENTATION

After the audit process is complete, the auditors should meet with the finance committee or governing board. Typically, this includes a presentation of the audit report and management comment letter. Auditors are available to answer any questions raised regarding the report or the process. They can clarify questions others may have regarding suggestions for improving processes. Following are some questions the board may consider asking the auditors in this setting:

- How did you assess the internal controls of the church and what weaknesses were detected?
- What are the most significant risks you believe we face as a church?
- In the review of the transaction processing, did you encounter any significant concerns?
- Do you have any reason to believe that temporarily restricted net assets are not being properly handled?

This meeting should also include an executive session time with the board or committee and the auditors. An executive session not only fulfills the requirements of some accountability groups, it is simply a best practice. This allows for the governance body that is ultimately responsible for the finances of the organization to have a candid discussion with the auditors as to their observations and potential concerns that may not have been voiced in a more public setting. Potential questions to address in this session are as follows:

- Did you receive the full cooperation of the staff and management?
- Do you have any concerns related to the competency of the staff?
- Do the audit adjustments present any concerns as to our systems or staff?
- Are there any additional items you would like to discuss in executive session?

As indicated earlier, the relationship a church has with its auditors should be a ministry partnership. However, as with any vendor, be sure to evaluate the firm you hired and your experience with your auditor after the process is complete. The audit committee could consider the following questions in assessing the completed audit engagement:

- Were the auditors responsive to the audit committee and to management?
- Did the auditors adequately discuss any changes in accounting and auditing standards?

- Was the management comment letter helpful in the operations of the church?
- Did the auditors appear objective in their interaction with, and evaluation of, management?
- Does the fee appear reasonable for the services and expertise provided?

The audit committee should consider input from management as well. Those closely involved in the audit will be able to provide a perspective on the competence, professionalism, and overall working relationship with the firm and staff.

The external audit is time consuming and is not a simple process. However, there are certainly benefits that exist. If the governing board/committee, management, and the auditors work together, the church will appreciate the results of this effort and improve how ministry is done in the future.

ACTION ITEMS

Business Administrator –
1. Be aware of, and comply with, applicable laws to avoid a compliance audit.
2. Plan to make an internal or external audit process run smoothly. Make sure that your accounting records are consistently in order and don't wait until audit time to "clean things up."
3. Work with your external auditors throughout the year when questions arise so that there are no surprises for you or the auditors after the year-end.

Senior Pastor –
1. Be aware of ways to avoid a compliance audit.
2. Be aware of the preparation required for an internal or external audit.
3. Be aware of the audit engagement progress and significant issues identified during the process.

Audit Committee/Board of Directors –
1. Churches can be impacted by the IRS and other regulatory agencies.
2. The board has a fiduciary responsibility over the organization.

Church boards often are very ministry focused and spend little time or have little expertise in the financial arena. Boards need to accept the responsibility to oversee internal or external audits. They must also have an understanding of issues that may lead to compliance audits.

Example 5.1: Sample Record Retention Policy

Sample Record Retention Policy

Many of the following items are now kept electronically. Be sure that your record retention policy recognizes the electronic media and addresses how long records should be kept and how they can be restored should the information be necessary to obtain in the future.

Document Destruction:

When records are no longer required to be maintained, a log of items destroyed will be signed off by two individuals. The records will be shredded after the dual verification is made. No records will be destroyed without the proper passage of time and approval of the department supervisor or the business administrator.

Accounting and Finance

Accounts payable ledgers and schedules	7 yrs.
Accounts receivable ledgers and schedules	7 yrs.
Audit reports	7 yrs, preferably permanently
Bank reconciliations	7 yrs.
Bank statements	7 yrs.
Budgets	6 yrs.
Checks (canceled)	7 yrs.
Duplicate deposit slips	2-5 yrs.
Depreciation schedules	5 yrs.
Financial statements (year-end, other optional)	Permanently
General ledgers, year-end trial balance	Permanently
Internal audit reports	7 yrs, preferably permanently
Inventories of products, materials, and supplies	7 yrs.
Invoices (to customers, from vendors)	7 yrs.
Journals	Permanently
Notes receivable ledgers and schedules	7 yrs.
Petty cash vouchers	3 yrs.
Physical inventory tags	3 yrs.
Purchase orders	1 yr.
Receiving reports	1 yr.
Requisitions	1 yr.
Sales records	7 yrs.
Investment transactions	7 yrs.

Contribution Records

Records of contributions	7 yrs.
Grants (un-funded)	1 yr.
Grants (funded)	7 yrs. after closure
Documents evidencing terms, conditions or restrictions on gifts	Permanently

Corporate Records

Annual Information Returns - Federal and State	Permanently
Contracts (expired)	7 yrs.
Debt agreements (current or expired)	Permanently
Deeds, mortgages, and bills of sale	Permanently
Insurance policies (expired)	3 yrs.
IRS or other Government Audit Records	Permanently
IRS Rulings	Permanently
Leases, expired	10 yrs.
Minute books of governing board and related committees	Permanently
Property appraisals by outside appraisers	Permanently
Property Insurance Policies	Permanently
Sales/Use Tax Records	7 yrs.
Tax-Exemption Documents and Related Correspondence	Permanently
Tax Returns	Permanently
Trademark registration and copyrights	Permanently

Payroll and Personnel Documents

Deduction Authorizations (after termination)	7 yrs.
Employee Earnings Records	Termination + 7 yrs.
Employee Handbooks	1 copy kept permanently
Employee Personnel Records	Termination + 7 yrs.
Employment applications	Termination plus 3-7 yrs.
Employment Contracts – Individual	Termination + 7 yrs.
Employment Records – All Non-Hired Applicants (including all applications and resumes – whether solicited or unsolicited, results of post-offer, pre-employment physicals, results of background investigations, if any, related correspondence)	2-4 yrs.
Garnishments, assignments, attachments	Termination + 7 yrs
I-9 Forms	3 yrs. after hiring or 1 yr. after separation if later
Payroll records & summaries	7 yrs.
Payroll Tax Records	7 yrs.
Personnel files (terminated)	7 yrs.
Retirement and pension records	Permanently
Time cards	7 yrs.
Unclaimed wage records (if not submitted to a state authority)	7 yrs.
W-2 and W-4 Forms	Termination + 7 yrs.

Example 5.2: Worker Classification

Worker Classification

The following questions were obtained from the Internal Revenue Service and are used to help identify the status of workers as either employees or independent contractors. According to the IRS, a "yes" answer to any of the following means the worker is an employee. For any individuals classified as independent contractors, documentation of that determination should be retained.

	Yes	No
1. Does the church provide instructions to the worker about when, where, and how he or she is to perform the work?	☐	☐
2. Does the church provide training to the worker?	☐	☐
3. Are the services provided by the worker integrated into the church's business operations?	☐	☐
4. Must the services be rendered personally by the worker?	☐	☐
5. Does the church hire, supervise, and pay assistants to the worker?	☐	☐
6. Is there a continuing relationship between the church and the worker?	☐	☐
7. Does the church set the work hours and schedule?	☐	☐
8. Does the worker devote substantially full-time to the business of the church?	☐	☐
9. Is the work performed on the church's premises?	☐	☐
10. Is the worker required to perform the services in an order or sequence set by the church?	☐	☐
11. Is the worker required to submit oral or written reports to the church?	☐	☐
12. Is the worker paid by the hour, week, or month?	☐	☐
13. Does the church have the right to discharge the worker at will?	☐	☐
14. Can the worker terminate his or her relationship with the church any time he or she wishes without incurring liability to the church?	☐	☐
15. Does the church pay the business or traveling expenses of the worker?	☐	☐

The following may indicate an independent contractor arrangement if all of the above were answered "no."

	Yes	No
16. Does the worker furnish significant tools, materials, and equipment?	☐	☐
17. Does the worker have a significant investment in facilities?	☐	☐
18. Can the worker realize a profit or loss as a result of his or her services?	☐	☐
19. Does the worker provide services for more than one firm at a time?	☐	☐
20. Does the worker make his or her services available to the general public?	☐	☐

Example 5.3: Sample Audit Preparation List

Sample Audit Preparation List

1. Please provide information on the risk assessment and internal controls of the organization including the internal control processes related to:
   a) Cash receipts
   b) Cash disbursements
   c) Payroll
   d) Computing environment related to the general ledger

2. Please sign the engagement letter and return the signed copy to us.

3. The audit committee chair, senior pastor, executive pastor, business administrator, and accounting and human resource staff will need to be available by phone or in person for an interview as required by Statements on Auditing Standards No. 99, Consideration of Fraud in a Financial Statement Audit. This can be scheduled in advance and worked around the various schedules of those individuals.

4. Provide written status of each prior year comment in the Management Comment Letter.

5. Please prepare confirmations for all cash, investment, and notes payable accounts.

6. Provide board minutes (including all subcommittees and attachments) for the year.

7. Complete information requested related to various tax issues of the church.

8. Provide information on any potential, pending, or threatening litigation or pending claims.

9. Please provide general ledger detail of all professional fees incurred year to date.

10. Please provide all new agreements entered into during the year.

11. Please provide copies of fund-raising information such as appeal letters and capital campaign literature.

12. Please provide listings of total reimbursed expenses and total credit card purchases for each of the pastoral staff and the business administrator.

13. Provide a listing of all nonrecurring journal entries recorded during the year.

14. Provide a detailed listing of website costs and support for financial information provided on the website.

15. Email the year-end trial balance before fieldwork starts.

16. Cash
    a) Provide a copy of the year-end bank reconciliations tying to the general ledger and the bank statement. All reconciliations should have a detailed listing of reconciling items.
    b) Provide a copy of all year-end bank statements and the subsequent month bank statements.
    c) Provide a schedule of all interbank transfers from five days prior to the fiscal year-end through five days subsequent to the fiscal year-end.

17. Investments
    a) Provide a copy of investment summary for the fiscal year.
    b) Provide copies of year-end investment statements.

18. Accounts Receivable
    a) Provide a copy of the year-end aging report
    b) Provide written analysis showing management's determination for adequacy.

Example 5.3: Sample Audit Preparation List (Cont.)

19. Inventory
    a) Provide an inventory detail listing tying to the general ledger.
    b) Provide information on significant new inventory purchases.

20. Prepaid Expenses – Provide a listing of prepaid expenses, supporting calculation for listed amounts, supporting documentation for significant amounts.

21. Property, Plant, and Equipment (Fixed Assets)
    a) Prepare a summary schedule and supporting detail schedule for all fixed assets and related accumulated depreciation.
    b) Provide a detailed listing of all additions (including construction in process) and pull support for all significant amounts.
    c) Provide a detailed listing of all retirements and related proceeds and pull support for all significant amounts.

22. Accounts Payable
    a) Provide a summary of accounts payable at year-end.
    b) Provide a check register for all checks written after year-end until the time of fieldwork.
    c) Provide a list of outstanding accounts payable to pastoral staff and management.
    d) Have available for review all unpaid invoices held as of execution fieldwork dates.

23. Accrued Expenses
    a) Provide a schedule for accrued wages for both salary and hourly staff.
    b) Provide accrued vacation listing, including names of employees, accrued hours, and rate used in accrual.

24. Debt, Including Lines of Credit
    a) Provide a schedule of debt as of year-end with information on the activity for the year and terms of the debt.
    b) Provide a statement from bank showing debt balance at year-end.
    c) Provide applicable amortization schedules.
    d) Provide a worksheet showing all loan covenants and that the organization and the status of the church's compliance at year-end.
    e) Provide a schedule of accrued interest expense.

25. Deferred Revenue – Provide a schedule showing deferred revenue by source.

26. Net Assets
    a) Provide a summary of net assets at year-end, including detailed activity in temporarily restricted accounts.
    b) Provide a year-end listing for board designated net assets and supporting documentation such as board minute references.

27. Revenue and Support
    a) Provide a reconciliation between the donor system contribution totals and the general ledger contribution accounts.
    b) Provide a program service revenue (child care, tuition, etc.) analytics summary using attendance data, fee rates, and general ledger revenue accounts. Please provide support for data used in analytics.

28. Expenses
    a) Provide a functional allocation of expense worksheets with all expenses allocated to ministry, administration, and fund-raising based on their use.
    b) Provide a reconciliation of quarterly 941 payroll reports to the general ledger salaries and wages accounts and have the 941 forms available for review.
    c) Provide a schedule listing all lease payments during the year and commitments for payments on those leases for the next five years.

Example 5.4: Closing Procedures Checklist

Closing Procedures Checklist

	Date	Initials	Frequency

1. **Cash (operating account)**
   a. Management receipt and review of bank statement — Monthly
   b. Record credit card fees — Monthly
   c. Record bank fees — Monthly
   d. Reconcile statement — Monthly
   e. Review reconciliation — Monthly

2. **Investments**
   a. Management receipt and review of broker statement — Monthly/Quarterly
   b. Record activity — Monthly
   c. Reconcile general ledger accounts with broker statement — Monthly
   d. Prepare monthly/quarterly investment activity summary — Monthly/Quarterly

3. **Accounts receivable**
   Determine if any modification to the allowance for doubtful accounts is necessary — Monthly

4. **Prepaid expenses**
   a. Update prepaid schedule — Monthly
   b. Make adjusting entry — Monthly
   c. Agree prepaid schedule to statement of financial position — Monthly

5. **Fixed assets**
   a. Roll fixed asset schedule at the beginning of the year — Annually
      1. Move additions from additions column to beginning cost column — Annually
      2. Delete disposals from schedule — Annually
      3. Move depreciation expense from the depreciation column and add to the beginning accumulated depreciation column — Annually
      4. Make sure beginning cost and beginning accumulated depreciation match the audit and your statement of financial position at the end of the prior fiscal year — Annually
   b. Add additions to schedule — Monthly
   c. Record depreciation expense — Monthly
   d. Record any deletions — Annually
   e. Agree fixed asset schedule to statement of financial position once changes are made — Monthly

Example 5.4: Closing Procedures Checklist (Cont.)

	Date	Initials	Frequency

6. **Inventory**
   a. Perform a physical inventory count — Annually
   b. Reconcile the general ledger balances to the physical count — Annually
   c. Review the inventory listing for obsolete items and adjust the general ledger balance as necessary — Annually

7. **Accounts payable**
   Agree accounts payable module to statement of financial position at end of month — Monthly

8. **Other accruals**
   a. Adjust payroll tax accrual — Monthly
   b. Record payroll accrual — At least annually
   c. Record vacation accrual — At least annually

9. **Long-term debt**
   Reconcile the general ledger liability account with statements — Monthly

10. **Temporarily restricted net assets**
    a. Review the temporarily restricted balances and make sure that they agree to prior year balances plus current year activity. — Annually
    b. If the software nets income and expenses through equity accounts to maintain these balances, an annual entry should be recorded to recognize the gross income and expenses. — Annually

11. **Revenue**
    a. Agree the donor system contributions amount to the general ledger contributions balance. — Monthly
    b. Determine that all noncash gifts have been recorded at their fair market value during the period — Monthly

12. **Expenses**
    Reconcile the payroll records to the Form 941s and W-2s — Quarterly/Annually

Example 5.5: Sample Internal Audit Preparation List

Sample Internal Audit Preparation List

Please prepare the following items prior to the internal audit. If you have questions, contact your auditor.

- ☐ Trial balance report
- ☐ Financial statements for the year
- ☐ Copies of any appeal letters or other communications for the year
- ☐ Copies of board and committee minutes for the year
- ☐ Please prepare a memo detailing the processes for recording and reporting cash receipts, cash disbursement, and payroll
- ☐ Copies of all current leases and contracts
- ☐ Provide files that include expense reimbursements for pastoral and management staff
- ☐ Provide files of corporate credit card payments during the year
- ☐ Provide information on any accounts that are not included in the general ledger (i.e. missions, women's ministries, parent teacher organization, etc.)
- ☐ Provide an analysis of current year to prior year income and expenses. Provide explanations for any variances of 10 percent or greater.
- ☐ Bank reconciliations and bank statements for the year (at least the last one of the year)
- ☐ Investment statements and reconciliations as of the end of the year
- ☐ Copy of the investment policy
- ☐ Aged listing of accounts receivable
- ☐ Analysis of doubtful accounts for accounts receivable
- ☐ Listing of notes receivable including information on the collectability
- ☐ Fixed asset schedule including beginning balance, purchases, disposals, ending balance, beginning accumulated depreciation, depreciation expense, depreciation disposal, and ending accumulated depreciation.
- ☐ Inventory listing by item with quantity, cost, and extended value
- ☐ Analysis of obsolete inventory items
- ☐ Aged listing of accounts payable
- ☐ Information on additional accruals such as payroll or vacation liabilities
- ☐ Information on any liabilities not included in the trial balance
- ☐ Listing of deferred revenue
- ☐ Note payable reconciliation and year-end statement
- ☐ Information on compliance with debt covenants
- ☐ Listing of temporarily restricted net assets and board designated net assets – including beginning balances, current year additions, current year releases, and ending balances
- ☐ Reconciliation of donor system totals for the year to the general ledger total of contributions
- ☐ Reconciliation of general ledger payroll amounts to quarterly Form 941s

Index

Index

Accountability, 2, 128, 132
Accounting Procedures Manual, 87, 90, 93, 115
Accounting records, 3, 86, 90, 94, 96, 100, 101, 111, 115, 126, 133
Administrative Board, 3, 68, 70, 72, 73, 74
Annual report, 72, 74
Audits, 75, 91, 92, 94, 95, 100, 118-140
    Compliance, 118-121
    Internal, 121-128, 130
    External, 128-133
Bank reconciliation, 108, 109, 110, 123, 134, 136, 140
Budgeting, 1, 3, 4, 5, 7, 10, 12-35
All-financial resources budget, 29
    Annual operating budget, 16, 21, 30, 32, 40, 45
    Bottom-up (participative), 14-16
    Capital-spending budget, 30-31
    Cash budget, 30-32
    Debt retirement budget, 30, 32, 33
    Incremental budgeting, 16, 17-20, 21, 28
    Program budgeting, 16-21, 23
    Top-down approach, 14-16
Budgets, 10, 11-18, 21, 24, 28, 31, 32, 43, 45, 70
Business Administrator, 3, 41, 52, 71, 74, 91, 132, 133, 134, 136
Cash disbursements, 28, 31, 87, 90, 92, 102, 104, 105, 106, 107
Cash reserve ratio, 49
Checks, 27, 92, 94, 96, 99, 100, 101, 105, 106, 107, 108, 110, 111, 115, 123, 131
Certified public accountant (CPA), 14, 75, 76, 94, 95, 115, 118, 122
Check authorization slip, 104-105, 115
Church accountant, 2, 64, 86
Church Business Administrator, 3, 52
Common costs, 18

Communication, 64, 67, 69, 70, 71, 119, 122, 128, 130, 131, 140
Compliance Audits, 118-120, 133
Contingency fund (reserve), 29
Contributions (offerings), 10-11, 15-16, 18, 21, 22, 25-28, 30, 31, 38-48, 51, 76, 92, 97-98, 100-102, 115, 119, 123, 127
    Cash (unrestricted), 28, 42, 43, 46, 47, 76, 77, 119
    Cash (restricted), 24, 27, 28, 30, 40, 44, 46, 47, 51, 127, 132, 137, 139, 140
    Giving units, 26
Counting committee, 89, 96, 100
Depreciation, 44, 45, 47, 83, 125, 128, 134, 136, 138, 140
Donated equipment, 5
Electronic Giving, 97
Embezzlement, 85, 86, 88, 91, 93, 94, 111
Expenditures, 2, 5, 16-19, 21-22, 28-32, 67, 75, 76, 103, 108, 111, 115
Finance Committee, 3-7, 9, 11-14, 22, 30, 65, 68, 70, 74, 87, 91
Financial Reporting, 2, 7, 27, 63-83, 90, 91, 118
    Principles of and other factors, 67-69
    To denominational offices and others, 71
    To general membership, 71
    To church management, 74
Financial reports, 2, 3, 13, 64-77, 86, 87, 91, 93, 99, 111, 115
Financial Secretary, 2-3, 89, 94, 100, 101, 103
Fixed cost, 12, 17
Insurance coverage, 94, 113, 115
Internal audit, 91, 95, 100, 101, 102, 108, 111, 115, 118, 121, 122-128
Internal controls, 85-116

Causes of problems, 87
For cash disbursements, 31, 87, 90, 92, 102-107, 115, 136
For cash receipts, 97-101
Objectives, 2, 5-23, 29, 48, 86
Separation of duties, 88, 94, 100, 101
Internal Revenue Service (IRS), 70, 71, 76, 91, 118, 135
Inventory, 48, 49, 56, 58, 112, 115, 125, 136, 139, 140
Mixed costs, 17
Offering envelopes, 72, 97, 99, 115
Online banking, 110
Online giving, 30, 97, 98, 107
Organization chart, 68
Pastor's discretionary fund, 24, 27, 28
Petty cash fund, 90, 99, 107, 111, 115
Planning, 5, 7-9, 10-18, 22, 28, 31-35, 64, 67
    Long-range planning, 9
    Master plan, 10
Pledges, 21-25, 29, 31, 87, 102, 122
Purchase orders, 102, 103, 115, 134
Ratios, 38, 39, 41, 43-51, 64
Reconciliation, 29, 107, 108-110, 113, 115, 123, 127, 134, 136, 137, 140
Reserve(s), 45, 47, 50, 127
Restrictive endorsements, 99
Revenue(s), 24, 29, 39, 47, 48, 54-60, 68, 70, 71, 74, 82, 126, 127
Slack, 21
Step costs, 17, 29
Treasurer, 2-3, 8, 11, 13, 24, 64-73, 77, 87, 90-100, 103-111, 115, 118, 119
Treasurer's manuals, 90
Volunteer(s), 4, 8, 25, 28, 70, 89, 91, 95, 103, 118, 121, 124, 128, 131

KEEP YOUR CHURCH WITHIN THE LAW

Newly Revised
Pastor, Church & Law
Complete 4-volume set now available

Pastor, Church & Law is the most comprehensive and practical legal reference for churches and clergy.

Get the answers you need quickly with legal briefs that give you an overview of the main points. Then dig deeper into each chapter for a more comprehensive look at each topic.

Richard Hammar answers all your legal questions about the church including: employment laws, liability, government regulations, property laws, first amendment issues, and more.

Volume 1: Legal Issues for Pastors
Richard Hammar uses court cases to help define and explain the legal distinction of ministerial status and its impact on laws that affect pastors and church boards. This 431-page volume addresses clergy employment contracts, compensation, termination, legal privileges and conditions of ministers, and the legal authority of ministers on behalf of the church. Also, the more common theories of clergy legal liability are reviewed.
Item #L417 | $29.95

Volume 2: Church Property & Administration
Dig deeper with Richard Hammar in this 525-page volume as he establishes the legal definition of the Church, and the relationship between the law and the Church. Topics covered include: inspection of records, federal reporting requirements, selection and liability of directors and officers, incorporation, church organization, zoning laws, and more.
Item #L416 | $29.95

Volume 3: Employment Law
Learn about employment laws and how they differ in application for churches in comparison to businesses. In this 319-page volume, Richard Hammar provides practical information and realistic examples on human resources topics including: hiring, discrimination, workers' compensation, immigration, termination, Fair Labor Standards Act, medical leave, and more.
Item #L415 | $29.95

Volume 4: Liability Church and State Issues
Learn which local, state, and federal laws and regulations apply to religious organizations and which ones do not. This 607-page volume addresses the church's legal liability on: negligent employee selection, retention, and supervision, counseling, breach of fiduciary duty, ratification, and defamation. Finally, Richard Hammar discusses the religion clause of the first amendment—its interpretation, inclusions, and exclusions.
Item #L414 | $29.95

Pastor, Church & Law 4th Edition
Complete 4-Volume Set: Item #L420S
$99.95 (More than a 15% savings)

Order online **YourChurchCatalog.com** • Order by phone **1-800-222-1840** • Sourcecode **S9DTB01**

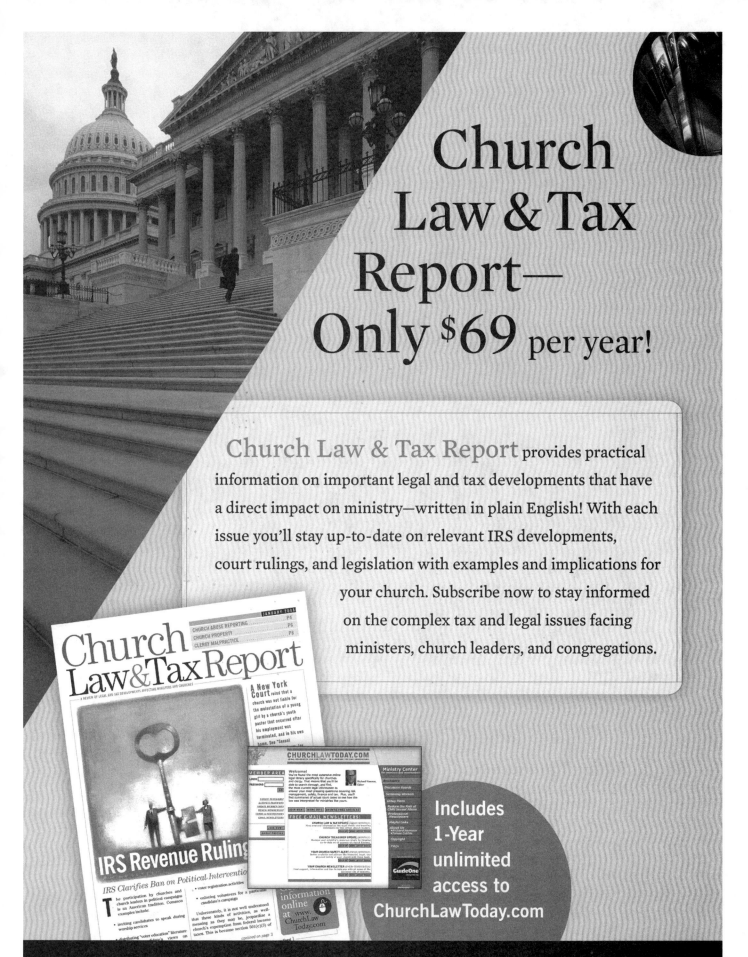